DEFINING
MOMENTS

Making Decisions That Will
Redefine Your Life

LORNE O. LIECHTY
WITH BRAD HOWARD

ENDORSEMENTS

We all have them! Moments in life that determine our future and help mold our destiny. Moments when we are forced to make a clear decision. In his book, *Defining Moments: Making Decisions That Will Redefine Your Life,* Lorne Liechty provides a framework that will help you respond in a godly way to the most critical apex moments of your life. When the road forks and you are required to choose a direction, this volume will help you attain the correct perspective and make the right choice. Actually, choosing to read this book will be one of your *defining moments.* Your life will never be the same.

–Dr. William M. Wilson
President, Oral Roberts University

Elizabeth Barrett Browning wrote, "Earth's crammed with heaven, and every common bush afire with God, but only he who sees takes off his shoes." In *Defining Moments*, Lorne Liechty, along with Brad Howard, prod us to be fully awake, on the lookout for God-orchestrated defining moments. Such moments indeed define us and set the trajectory for our future. The authors write as life coaches, unpacking vital biblical principles peppered with real-life stories. The quality of our lives is determined by the quality of our choices. You will learn in these pages how to recognize, analyze, and correctly respond to life's defining moments. Readers are also challenged to make the most of "micromoments" that condition us to respond with courage to life's defining moments. This incisive book also provides clear steps of action. *Defining Moments* is an invitation to life on a higher plane. A pivotal, defining moment for you may well be to just keep reading this book. What you discover in these pages can redefine your life.

–David Shibley
Founder, Global Advance

It is an honor and privilege for me to recommend Lorne Liechty's newest book, *Defining Moments.* I have known him for years, both professionally and personally, and this manuscript lays out a process to redefine your life while making critical decisions with confidence.

The history of the Bible tells us that God has always had a connection between the physical and spiritual realm, each major move of God is accompanied with a financial blessing too. This book has practical steps for making life-changing decisions through the filter of biblical and business principles. These choices can be made in personal, business, and spiritual areas of life to help create the defining moments we desire. It is a must read for every stage of life.

–Larry Huch
Senior Pastor, DFW New Beginnings Church

Lorne Liechty is a successful lawyer and now a writer of a practical and important book for both the younger and older generations. In it he guides people to make important, right, and wise decisions that will bless their lives and the community they are a part of. Lorne has touched on topics like decisions related to marriage, to schooling, to business, and to friendship.

Our lives are full of crossroads that call on us to make serious and sober decisions. I wish I had a book like Lorne's when I was a teenager, and again when I attended college, and again when I choose what car to buy! I recommend that you buy the book *Defining Moments*, and read it all the way through the first time. Then, don't put this book away as you would any other book (except your Bible). Put it on your desk or keep it on the table next to your bed. When you wake up in the night and ponder the next day's decisions, pick up Lorne's book and read the chapter that deals with each decision. Then pray to God for wisdom to follow the wise advice that Lorne gives you. I am planning to do the same!

–Joseph Shulam
Author, and Founder,
Netivyah Bible Instruction Ministry

Through instruction and wonderful stories, Lorne has brilliantly uncovered the importance of identifying and leveraging your defining moments. Reading this book could quite possibly be one of them.

–Dr. Mark K. Mullaney
Senior Pastor, Jesus First Transformation
Warehouse, Albuquerque, NM

DEDICATION

This book is dedicated to the individuals who have helped shape my life by being examples to me, and to those who have helped me with critical decisions in my life. Those people are too numerous to name, and many of their names have faded from my memory, but the following people would certainly be included in that group:

Paul H. Liechty and Shirley Jean Liechty, my parents.

Paul E. Liechty, my older brother.

James P. Syvrud, my brother-in-law.

Dr. Alan F. Repko (Oral Roberts University).

Pastor Harold May, who led me to accept Christ as my Savior.

Pastor Thomas Murphy (Gospel Center Missionary Church, Mishawaka, Indiana).

Pastor Larry Lea, who taught me to pray.

Kevin P. McGinnis, my law partner for over thirty years, who walked with me through many difficult times, and celebrated many great successes with me.

My uncles Harley Carlson, Ezra Liechty, and Silas Liechty.

CONTENTS

PREFACE

I have practiced law for forty years. During that time, I have had the opportunity to see and experience a wide variety of human behavior. One thing I have observed is that so many people lack basic, good decision-making skills. I frequently see people get themselves into difficult situations as a result of bad decisions. This book is written as a guide to help you make good decisions in the future.

The inspiration for this book came from a sermon series titled *Defining Moments* that my pastor, Brad Howard, delivered in early 2020. I had just written an article about an event that radically changed my life in one of our local papers, and Brad used a quote from it in his initial message in that series. That Sunday morning, I realized that the concept of *Defining Moments* was larger than my article and larger than Brad's sermon series. I proposed the idea of this book to Brad at breakfast a few days later and, as is his way, Brad was 100 percent supportive and agreed to help me with it.

Our goal in writing this book is to provide a pathway for everyone, Christian and non-Christian, to make good decisions when they are facing *Defining Moments* in their lives. However, as Christians, we believe that biblical principles are the foundation for our civilization and provide a guide for our lives and, therefore, you will see many references to the Bible throughout the book. President Ronald Reagan once said that, "Within the covers of the Bible are the answers for all the problems men face," and the biblical stories and principles included provide great examples for illustrating the principles set out in this book.

I have always felt that I have been blessed with extraordinary life experiences. I have been fortunate to meet and interact with many very intelligent, successful, and sometimes famous people. I thank God for the life He has given me. Many of the stories in this book come from my personal experience, and some of the stories come from Brad's life experiences. Hopefully intermingling those stories is not too confusing.

Brad Howard has been my pastor since 1996, and has been the best "pastor" that I have ever had. He has been a mentor and spiritual companion for the past twenty-five years. During this time we have had good times and tense times, but I have always recognized his spiritual leadership in my life, and Brad has always trusted my advice. I am grateful for his assistance and encouragement in writing this book, and will always be grateful for his leadership and his friendship.

The stories of several of my friends are included, although the names have often been changed. These stories are shared to provide guidance and illustrate principles in the book, and I hope that all of those individuals are pleased with the result.

Finally, I must thank my wife, Mary, for her encouragement and support during this project. Mary is a true Proverbs 31 woman, and my life would never have been what it is without her.

–Lorne O. Liechty

CHAPTER I

Beginning Moments

"The man who views the world at 50 the same as he did at 20,
has wasted 30 years of his life."

—Muhammad Ali[1]

I walked away from the crowd and the late-night excitement to look for my parents. I had a sick feeling in my stomach that I was embarrassed to explain to them or anyone else. It's amazing to think that something so inconsequential can put an imprint on your life that you can still feel more than fifty years later.

I learned the impact of Defining Moments as a naive eleven-year-old farm boy. Growing up on a small family farm, money was a very limited commodity, much different than the wheat we raised and the milk and eggs we produced. As a child, I didn't interact with money regularly, and consequently, I hadn't learned how to use it wisely. However, we were taught to work hard, and when you were paid fifteen cents an hour for field work, you had to work a long time to accumulate anything. I had saved $65 when the carnival arrived for a three-day stop at our hometown's seventy-fifth anniversary. I was excited by the rides and bright lights, but I was mesmerized by the games of chance. I was certain I could throw a softball and knock over three milk bottles, throw a ring around one of fifty Coke bottles fastened to a wooden base, and pop three balloons with four darts, and I was willing to put down my hard-earned money to prove it. When the carnival left town, all I had to show for my efforts was a homely blue stuffed dog and empty pockets, and to this day I still remember the sick feeling in the pit of my stomach. I was broke and wouldn't have any more money until the end of the summer. The lesson I learned was reflected in my New Year's resolutions six months later (1968), which started with, "Be a miser," and also included, "Put money in bank," and, "Don't take money out of bank." I had squandered my life savings, but had learned a lesson that would impact how I managed my money the rest of my life!

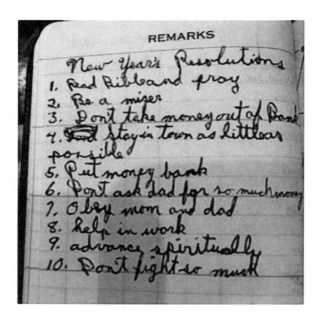

MORE THAN A MOMENT

A Defining Moment has been described in many ways. According to one source, the term was first used in the early 1980s, and is defined as, "a point at which the essential nature or character of a person, group, etc., is revealed or identified."[2] However, that is a static definition, and does not emphasize what is most important—the *consequences* of a Defining

Moment. If a moment only "reveals" or "identifies" our essential nature, it is no more than a signpost telling the world who we are.

In this book, we will focus primarily on two things. First, we will address how to Recognize, Analyze, and Respond Effectively (the acronym "RARE") to Defining Moments in our lives. It is important that we understand this process so that those critical decision points in our lives don't simply pass us by.

Second, we will look at the *changes* that can result in our character from encountering Defining Moments, and the impact those Defining Moments can have on our lives. We want to use the RARE process to convert those moments into points at which our essential nature or character *can be* established or changed. Those moments should not just reveal or identify our character; rather, we should use those experiences to *form* and *shape* our identity and character. We want to focus on the transformative power of those moments and how we can walk through them to become the people God wants us to be.

A Defining Moment can be an achievement or a failure, something you do or something you go through; but you will know you have experienced a Defining Moment if you are a different person after you have been through it. You can go through a tension-packed, life-threatening experience that does not change your character. Such an experience does nothing to truly define who you are. Conversely, you can go through something as simple as losing $65 to a carnival barker, and it can define essential character traits for the rest of your life.

Unfortunately, so often in life we encounter a potential Defining Moment but we fail to recognize, analyze, or react effectively to it, and the opportunities it presents are lost forever. What could have been a life-changing moment becomes simply a lost opportunity. As Christians, we know that our lives are more than just a series of unguided experiences. God put us here for a reason—to grow and develop into people who are walking in the image of God, and to shape our character in a manner that reflects His love to everyone we meet. He brings us to experiences that will allow us to be conformed into His image and to become the people He wants us to be. But if we fail to recognize them, analyze them or react effectively to them, or fail to really change through those experiences, they become nothing more than faint memories and lost opportunities.

The purpose of this book is to help people recognize those key points in our lives, analyze and respond to them effectively, and develop into the people God wants us to be—people who will maximize all of the experiences and opportunities that are presented to us.

THINGS CAN CHANGE YOUR LIFE WITHOUT CHANGING YOU

Let's be clear about one thing, however: not everything that changes the course of your life is a Defining Moment, because not everything that changes your life changes you. That is true for a lot of reasons. Sometimes we fail to recognize what is going on; sometimes we fail to use a Defining Moment in our lives to make the changes that could have resulted from the opportunity; *and sometimes things just happen!*

At age 16, I was carefree, and loved nothing more than riding my dirt bike—a sparkling blue 1971 Honda SL 350 that would have climbed a straight wall if I had the guts to try it. When it was warm enough, and sometimes when it wasn't, I spent all of my free time riding trails and riding around town. I was a nominal Christian, raised in a three-times-a-week, church-going family, but not real serious about my faith. Although generally unconcerned about the future (like most boys that age), my post-high school plan was to attend North Dakota State University, home of *The Bison*, join the skydiving club, study history, and spend the rest of my life as a high school history teacher in my home state of North Dakota.

All this changed on a drizzly Easter Sunday morning in 1972. Riding my dirt bike home from church that morning, a car suddenly turned left in front of me and my motorcycle collided broadside into the car. I went airborne over the car, landed against a curb in a muddy pool of water, and by the grace of God ended up with only a crushed ankle, which put me in the hospital for three weeks. More importantly, it caused me to spend the summer incapacitated, with a cast the entire length of my left leg. But for that accident, I would have spent another summer as a migrant worker, following the wheat harvest from Oklahoma back to North Dakota.

However, because of that accident, the direction of my life was changed forever. That summer I met a girl at a Bible camp meeting in my hometown. As you might imagine, I was smitten and was convinced that this girl was probably *the one*. However, that young lady had no intention of staying in North Dakota after high school, and left the state to attend college. After one long three-month quarter at NDSU (where I was told that the broken leg I suffered in the motorcycle accident prevented me from skydiving), I transferred to Oral Roberts University in Tulsa, Oklahoma, because it was closer to Kansas City, where that young lady was attending college. Unfortunately (or fortunately?), within a month after transferring, that relationship crashed and slowly burned out.

My plan had been to stay in North Dakota and teach high school history, but God had a different plan for my life. While attending ORU I decided to become an attorney, met my wife, met my law partner, and never came close to teaching high school history classes!

―――――――

It would be tempting to say that the motorcycle accident was a Defining Moment in my life, but was it really? Clearly the direction of my life was changed forever. But that in and of itself does not satisfy the criteria for a Defining Moment. The direction of my life was changed, but I wasn't changed. As stated at the beginning of this chapter, one of the critical elements of a Defining Moment in our lives is that our essential character is established or changed. After the accident, I was still a carefree (and often careless) teenage boy, and a nominal, church-going Christian who still wasn't real serious about my faith. That accident did nothing to make me evaluate the direction of my life or my character. Except for a few scars and a minor loss of mobility, I was essentially the same person after the accident that I was before it; I just happened to be pointed in a different direction.

THE BEFORE-AND-AFTER TEST

When we encounter a true Defining Moment in our life, it has the power to change us and change our character. Those changes are built into the term itself; these are *moments* that *define* who we are. The Bible is full of stories like this, stories of people who are brought to moments where they have to make a decision, and that decision will change who they are, how they are perceived by their community, and often, will change the course of their lives. One of my favorites is the story of Joshua and Caleb and their return from the land of Canaan in the book of Numbers, chapters 13 and 14.

To understand and analyze the impact of a Defining Moment in a person's life, you need to examine that person both before and after the moment. Although the Bible does not discuss the early lives of either Joshua or Caleb, they were certainly born in Egypt prior to the Israelites' exodus. Growing up and living their early years under Egyptian slavery and bondage would have certainly impacted them for the remainder of their lives. Joshua must have been recognized as a man of great valor and military prowess, because early in the forty-year pilgrimage from Egypt to the Promised Land, Moses chose Joshua to lead the first major military battle that Israel faced.[3] The Israelites had travelled only a short period of time to a place called Rephidim, which may have been in the Sinai wilderness or maybe even in modern-day

Saudi Arabia.[4] Moses told Joshua to, "Choose us out men, and go out, fight with Amalek . . ."[5]

Further, Joshua ministered to Moses and went with him to Mount Sinai and waited while Moses ascended to the top of the mount and received the Ten Commandments and other key portions of the Mosaic law from God.[6] All of this shows us that Joshua had developed into a man of character prior to his ultimate Defining Moment. However, despite these early references to Joshua in the book of Exodus, there is nothing to indicate that either he or Caleb would become the men they were to become—but one Defining Moment would change that forever.

As the Israelites approached the Promised Land, God told Moses to choose one ruler from each tribe of Israel to search out the land that there were about to enter. Joshua, from the tribe of Ephraim, and Caleb, from the tribe of Judah, were two of those twelve men. The twelve men crossed into the land of Canaan for the express purpose of spying on the land to see if the people in the land were strong or weak, few or many, whether the land was good or bad; whether the cities they inhabited were like camps or strongholds; whether the land was rich or poor; and whether or not there were forests. This reconnaissance mission was to be into a hostile land and needed to be done without warning to its inhabitants, and the success of the mission was critical to the future of the Israelite people.

The twelve spies were very successful. They were gone forty days and returned to Moses, Aaron, and the entire congregation, and gave their report. And what a report it was! They brought back the fruit of the land of Canaan and confirmed that the land indeed was a land that flowed with milk and honey. But now each of those twelve men was faced with the moment of truth, and ten of them failed the test. The majority report was that the people of the Promised Land were like giants and were too strong for the Israelites (and implicitly too strong for God) to conquer.

Caleb and Joshua, however, did not accept the majority report. The Bible tells us that Caleb stepped up and quieted the people before Moses and said, "Let us go up at once and take possession, for we are well able to overcome it."[7] While Caleb was the speaker, we can be confident that Joshua stood with Caleb. All the other ten spies died by a plague, but Caleb and Joshua survived[8] and were blessed. Of all the adult men that came out of Egypt, only Caleb and Joshua were allowed to enter into the Promised Land, because "they have wholly followed the Lord."[9]

From that moment forward, the lives of these two great men changed. They became unquestioned leaders in the nation of Israel, they led the Israelites to conquer the land of Canaan, and they were rewarded for their faith in God. Joshua became the leader of Israel after Moses' death, and was blessed by God's promise that no man would be able to stand against him and that God would be with him as he was with Moses. Caleb also became a conquering hero of Israel and was rewarded with the land of Hebron as his inheritance. He led the Tribe of Judah, which led the nation of Israel into battle, conquering the land of Canaan after Joshua's death.

I am sure that when the ten spies delivered the *majority report*, Joshua and Caleb felt pressure to go along with the crowd. The easy course would have been to do so and to say that the Canaanites were too much for the nation of Israel—but they did not choose the easy course. Instead they chose to put their faith and trust in God and His promises and said to go forward—and history records that they were correct, even if it took another forty-plus years to prove that out. They came to a Defining Moment, they recognized what it was, analyzed the possible responses, and chose to trust in God and take the risks that came with it. That is a true Defining Moment and an effective response, and that is what each of us should strive for when confronted with similar situations.

BE CAREFUL WHAT YOU ASK FOR

Unfortunately, however, the failure to recognize, analyze, and respond effectively to Defining Moments can also cause us to miss those opportunities and to miss the best that God has for us in our lives. The

Bible gives us many examples showing where the wrong choices were made. One of the clearest of those moments, and maybe one of the most relevant for twenty-first century Christians, is the story of the rich young ruler, which is found in three of the Gospels.[10]

The Bible doesn't say a lot about who this person was, but we know that he was wealthy and a man of significance (a "ruler" in Luke 18:18). It is also evident from the story that he was a godly man who sought to be even closer to God. In fact, in the book of Mark, it says that he came running to see Jesus and knelt before Him to show that he honored Him as more than just another "Good Teacher," as he called Jesus. It is important to grasp the significance of this moment. Here was a man who had followed God all his life, but was seeking to go from good to great. He wanted so intently to follow God's will in his life that he came running up to Christ and asked what he must do to obtain eternal life. It may be as clear of an example as we have in the Bible of a Defining Moment! The young ruler was asking what was necessary to change his essential character and what he could do to become a different person.

But unfortunately this may also be as clear of an example as exists in the Bible of the consequences of not responding effectively in a Defining Moment. The rich young ruler is seeking the path to eternal life, and Jesus tells him to keep the commandments.[11] When the young ruler answers that he has kept the commandments from the time he was a child, the Bible says that Jesus loved him and told him there was only one more thing he had to do—"sell whatever you have and give to the poor, and you will have treasure in heaven; and come, take up the cross and follow Me."[12] There it was. The Defining Moment of this young man's life was served up on a platter. All he had to do was follow Christ's instruction and he would be forever changed. Unfortunately, rather than follow those divine instructions, the young man walked away sorrowfully, because he had many possessions. Who knows what course his life would have taken if he had only followed these instructions? We could guess and speculate, but what we do know is that by responding incorrectly, he missed God's will for his life.

This story has incredible relevance today. In our American churches there are many people who are wealthy (especially compared to people around the world) and who keep (or seek to keep) the commandments. Further, in prayer we often ask God for direction for our lives. While it seems that we rarely are given such direct answers to our questions as the young ruler was given to his (or maybe we're just not listening?), each of us is confronted from time to time with similar Defining Moments, opportunities and decision points in our lives. The goal and purpose of this book is to help each of us to recognize, analyze, and respond effectively to those moments so that we, unlike the rich young ruler, are able to maximize the life-changing opportunities that are available to us.

IMPACT UPON EVERYTHING

All my life I have heard people say things like, "Don't limit God," and that is certainly true when we discuss the topic of Defining Moments. When we encounter a life-changing moment, we have no way of knowing the breadth of its impact upon us. It can, *and probably will,* change us *personally, professionally,* and *spiritually.* There may be no greater example of this than Peter. When he met Christ and took Him up on His offer to, "Follow Me," Peter instantly began a road of thorough transformation of mind, body, and spirit. *Personally*, he went from being impulsive and scared of men's responses, to being the steadfast rock upon whom Christ would build His Church. *Professionally*, he went from being a fisherman with a definable career path, to being a fisher of men, an undefined career with no prior path to follow. *Spiritually*, he went from being a Jew with an unknown commitment to his faith, to becoming a Spirit-filled follower of Christ who was willing to suffer martyrdom for his Savior. Later in this book, we will look at how we can be transformed in all these facets of our lives. For now, it is important to recognize that when God confronts us with a moment of decision, we need to be prepared to go wherever He wants to take us, because those decisions can impact every aspect of our lives.

It is important to note that Defining Moments are not limited to individuals. Companies, churches, and nonprofit organizations frequently confront Defining Moments, and their ability to recognize, analyze, and respond effectively in those circumstances can have the same significance to the future of those organizations as it has to an individual. That is why it is so important to have leaders in those organizations who are trained and capable of making good decisions.

We faced a Defining Moment in the life of our church in the summer of 2001. Lakeshore Assembly of God Church began meeting in 1991 in a tiny strip shopping center storefront in Rowlett, Texas. In 1994, Brad Howard was installed as senior pastor of the church, with a tiny congregation of about fifty. Brad's entry into Lakeshore signaled a new day, and God blessed the church and it began to grow. In 1997, Lakeshore moved out of its storefront location into a real church building in Rockwall, Texas, and God continued to bless and the church continued to grow. It didn't take long for God to fill our little church building, and we spent several years trying to manage the facility to handle maximum-capacity crowds in three services, while looking for a new location that would serve our rapidly growing congregation.

Brad had a vision for a church campus that would be large enough to facilitate multiple buildings, with athletic fields and a stream flowing through it; and the vision was so clear that he took the time to sketch it out as a guide for our property search team.

The clear vision was a blessing, but a property like that which fit within our budget was not an easy thing for a small church to find in a booming community just outside Dallas. But finally, after months of diligently searching, we found a fifty-acre site with a beautiful pond on a major thoroughfare just three miles south of Rockwall. The property was perfect for our church and had an affordable asking price.

Our church was at a decision point that would be a Defining Moment for our congregation. Moving to that property would change the essential character of our church. Brad's excitement was infectious, and after the elders toured the site, it seemed like this was a fulfillment of Brad's vision—until it was time for the vote. Brad was devastated when the elders voted not to buy the property. Even more stunning was that the elders' rejection of the property was based upon my recommendation! At the time, it seemed that a Defining Moment and a great opportunity had inexplicably passed us by.

CHAPTER 2

Stumbling Blocks

"In a higher world it is otherwise, but here below to live is to change, and to be perfect is to have changed often."

— JOHN HENRY CARDINAL NEWMAN[1]

After reading the last chapter, you might wonder how Brad and I restored our relationship to the point where we were able to write this book together. Without more explanation, it would appear that I had just torpedoed Brad's vision for our church. Many questions could be asked: Was Brad's vision consistent with God's, or was he missing it? Was Lorne *that elder* in their church—you know, the elder that needs to exert his perceived power to control the church or the pastor? Did this decision cause a split in the church? Did they find another property that fit the church's needs? Did Brad and Lorne have to seek counseling?

Fortunately, the answer to all of those questions is "No," and the story has a happy ending. At the time there was no doubt that Lakeshore needed a new facility. Its existing facility had been built nearly one hundred years earlier, and had served as the home for multiple denominations and congregations over the years. While it had a quaint, *small town, country church* style, the church building did not have adequate parking, office space, classrooms for Sunday school or space for a children's or youth ministry, and it had a leaky basement. As an interim step, the church had tried utilizing a nearby facility, but that had proven to be nothing short of a disaster.

However, Lakeshore had also recently experienced a number of changes in the eldership, staff, and membership, which led to corresponding fluctuations in our congregation. For those reasons and others, including a good dose of what I hoped was guidance from the Holy Spirit, I was convinced that the church was not yet ready to take on the financial burden of purchasing the land and borrowing the money necessary to construct a new sanctuary. A decision to move forward too quickly could lead to financial disaster, and the potential collapse of our church.

The challenge was how to stop, or at least slow down, the process while recognizing Brad's leadership and spiritual authority and not denying the vision God had given to him. In order to properly address this concern, I went to Brad prior to raising my concern with the board of elders. Based upon our prior relationship, Brad had confidence that I would only raise these concerns if I was sure that they were valid. Our relationship of mutual respect and trust allowed us to continue to work together despite the potential for irreconcilable conflict that surrounded the decision not to purchase the new property.

Lakeshore Church remained in its tiny facility, and the congregation once again grew to its breaking point. During that same time, the church's finances stabilized, new staff members were added to strengthen the infrastructure of the church, and Brad grew into new levels of leadership and pastoral maturity. All those things made our church much stronger only one year later, when I went to Brad to discuss finding a new facility for our church. Miraculously, and I mean that literally, despite the explosive growth in the Rockwall area, the property that Brad believed was the fulfillment of his vision was still for sale, and the owner was willing to sell it to the church for the same price as we had negotiated more than a year before, *even though the fair market value had increased by nearly 50 percent!* Needless to say, the church purchased the property, built a new sanctuary, and continues to worship and thrive there today, more than fifteen years and multiple remodels and expansions later. Despite other occasional disagreements over the years, Brad is still the senior pastor, I am still a member of the board of elders, and we remain friends.

This was a Defining Moment in the life of Lakeshore Church and significantly altered the direction of the church. Brad and the elders recognized the moment, evaluated its potential impact on the church, and responded effectively. As a result, Lakeshore Church was forever changed for the better, our ministry efforts have continued to grow, and our impact upon our community has expanded.

The story, and its conclusion, illustrate many things that we need to consider when discussing the topic of Defining Moments. We have noted how important it is to recognize, analyze, and respond effectively to Defining Moments. But like so many things in life, there are rarely simple, or clear, *yes or no* responses. There are always nuances that need to be considered when evaluating those moments. Things like how those decisions will affect our futures and the futures of others impacted by them; how we apply God's wisdom to our evaluation and responses; our prior inertia and resistance to change (negative inertia); and timing. Analyzing and responding effectively requires a recognition of those nuances and the wisdom to address them. We will examine many of these issues on a more detailed basis later in this book.

BE WILLING TO REJECT PRECONCEIVED IDEAS

This principle may seem obvious, but it isn't easy. We all tend to make decisions based upon what we believe is right. These preconceived ideas can keep us from responding effectively to situations that could be our Defining Moments. We need to approach these opportunities and decisions with an open mind and a willingness to hear from God. Remember the story of the rich young ruler? He may have been expecting congratulations for his lifetime of obeying the commandments, and certainly was not expecting the answer he received from Jesus. That is shown by his response. Yet because he was not willing to reject his preconceived ideas and accept what Jesus was telling him, he missed all the blessings that God had in store for him if he would have been obedient.

The opposite is shown by the story of Lakeshore Church's move. The pastor's preconceived idea was that the new property was right for the church and that they should move forward with the purchase immediately. However, when confronted with a conflicting opinion, he did not turn away like the rich young ruler, but rather was willing to set aside his preconceived notions and consider that God had a different plan for the church. As a result of his willingness to consider other opinions and counsel,[2] the church had the opportunity to stabilize before moving. God still blessed Brad and the church with the fulfillment of his vision. We don't know what would have happened if Brad would have pushed the elders to approve the purchase of the property the first time; but we do know that despite the delay, by setting aside his preconceived ideas, the church was able to move to the new property in a healthier condition and that it has thrived ever since. As the old proverb says, the proof is in the pudding.

When confronted with a decision that can be a Defining Moment in your life, you need to be willing to confront that decision with an open mind. If you are unwilling to consider other options, the decision you are facing may not become a Defining Moment in your life because it is likely you will proceed along your prior course and will not be changed by the moment. However, if you are willing to review and analyze the decision based upon biblical input and wise, diverse counsel, you will be in a position where you are willing to let God guide you and direct you to the place He wants you to go. Too often, however, people simply choose to follow their preconceived ideas and make decisions based upon how they have acted in the past and in reliance on their own ideas rather than sound, godly insight and advice. In doing so, people often fail to implement the RARE principles, and therefore miss the opportunity to grow and be changed.

BE WILLING TO CHANGE

One thing we need to remember when considering Defining Moments is that to some extent we are all resistant to change. The formal term for this is *inertia*, which can be defined as "indisposition to motion, exertion, or change."[3] Or, as stated in Newton's first law of motion, an object at rest stays at rest and an object in motion stays in motion unless acted on by an external force. Some people resist change so much that it is nearly impossible to move forward, and for others it is less of an influence—but it affects all of us to some extent. While not proper scientific terminology, it can be useful for illustrative purposes to use the term *negative inertia* to indicate that our resistance to change can have a negative impact upon us.

God intends for all of us to continue growing throughout our lives, and growth requires change. Yet one of the things that is most amazing about the concept of inertia in our personal lives is that we often remain resistant to change even if we are unhappy, or sometimes miserable, in our daily lives! That seems so incongruous. Why would we resist making changes if we are unhappy in our current situations? And yet it's true, and oftentimes it seems that as a person's dissatisfaction (or even misery) increases, that person becomes less willing to change.

However, the reality is that nothing is as painful as staying stuck somewhere you don't belong. If you are stuck in a rut, you can rock back and forth, but you will go nowhere. Rather than accomplishing something, you become weary and worn down, leaving no energy to move forward. When you are bound by negative inertia, you also don't respond well to the world around you. You tend to live by your feelings rather than by faith, you get offended easily, and you generally have a negative outlook because you are unhappy and are not experiencing the *joy unspeakable* that the Bible says we should experience when living by faith.[4]

There are many reasons why people resist changes, but three common reasons are comfort, lack of knowledge, and fear.

1. *Comfort.* Regardless of the situations we are in, sooner or later we learn how to deal with them and manage our day-to-day lives. Eventually, we get comfortable as things get more familiar, regardless of the situation we are in. When we get comfortable the need to change seems less urgent and we are less likely to take the risk. This comfort can cause us to be so unaware of our true situation that only a change will help. Sometimes it seems like you don't know how much your situation hurts until you get out of it.

2. *Lack of knowledge.* We often fail to change because we do not understand what other options are available to us, or we don't even know those other options exist. This is one reason why seeking good counsel from a diverse group of wise friends and advisors is so valuable. Other people can bring their experiences to bear and suggest options that we never would have considered.

3. *Fear.* Fear may be the strongest factor keeping us from changing, and fear comes in many forms. We often fear the unknown—what will result from a change? We fear failure—what if we take steps to change our lives but are unsuccessful in our new ventures? We fear leaving our friends, family, and colleagues—changes that result from Defining Moments may require us to leave people we know and like and to establish new relationships. The need to interact with new people can be accompanied by the fear of being unable to make friends or build good relationships in those new situations.

Those factors of comfort, lack of knowledge, and fear must be overcome, however. When we are confronted with Defining Moments, accepting the challenges and opportunities those moments provide will always require change at some level. Remember that *change* is built into the very definition of a Defining Moment: a Defining Moment is a point at which the essential character of a person is established or *changed*. Simply put, if we are unwilling to change, we will not realize the full benefits that God has in store for us from the Defining Moments we encounter. We need to get out of our ruts, overcome the negative inertia in our lives, and maximize the opportunities that lie before us. Only then can we truly experience that life of *joy unspeakable and full of glory* that God calls us to.

A willingness to change was evident in the decision to move our church to a new property. At first blush, it may seem that the initial decision by our elders to not purchase the property was just resisting the change that eventually came. We were in a miserable situation (stuck in a rut), with a building that was too small and not capable of serving our growing congregation, but it was working well enough that we could have easily continued in that situation and survived. Maybe we were comfortable in that rut; maybe we didn't have enough information about what it would take to build a new church and what the benefits would be to our church; and maybe we were afraid of what the future in a new location held, afraid that we would not be able to pay the costs necessary to build a new building, or afraid that we would not succeed. But in fact, after the initial decision not to proceed and after our church had stabilized, the elders showed that they were willing to change and accept the challenge that came with those changes, and it has proven to be an extremely successful change. God used that Defining Moment to change the future of our church!

BE READY TO RECOGNIZE OPPORTUNITIES

If we recognize the Defining Moments that we encounter, we will be more likely to make good decisions and maximize the positive impacts to our lives that can result from those moments. Unfortunately, we tend not to look for life-changing moments in our lives, and therefore often do not recognize them when they confront us. There are many reasons we miss the significance of those moments. It can be as simple as the fact that while living our day-to-day lives we do not expect major life-changing moments to confront us (although even small decisions can lead to Defining Moments, as we will discuss in chapter 8). Or it can be that we miss Defining Moments because we do not want to face them and the decisions that accompany them—we choose to willfully ignore the opportunities facing us.

So how do we recognize when we are facing Defining Moments in our lives? Each instance is likely to be different, as evidenced by the examples given in this book, but there are some general principles to consider when evaluating these situations.

First, if we want to recognize these turning points, we need to acknowledge and understand that they exist, and be on the lookout for them. Defining Moments often involve significant decisions in our lives, including areas of our spiritual, personal, and professional lives. Some decisions are easy to identify as Defining Moments. For example, facing a decision to get married or to make a major career change. These major crossroad points should be readily apparent to all of us. It is more difficult to recognize those Defining Moments which involve decisions seemingly less material, yet often those seemingly immaterial decisions can also have a major impact shaping our character and changing the direction of our lives. If we are attuned to looking for significant moments in our lives, we are more likely to recognize them, even the less obvious ones.

Second, if we as Christians want to maximize our Defining Moments, it is important that we are attentive to God's Word and are hearing His voice. It is God's will for us to grow and mature spiritually through the Defining Moments we encounter. To do that, we need to discern His will. In Isaiah 30:21, it says that our ears shall hear a word behind us, telling us the way, and that we should walk in it when we turn to the right and to the left. When we are confronted with true Defining Moments, our lives are about to change and our direction will shift, sometimes to the right or to the left, *and sometimes we will do a complete 180!* As that verse indicates, God will show us when we approach those points. We are more likely to hear His voice clearly when we are walking close to Him.

Finally, one indication that you are facing a Defining Moment is that the decision you are making may require you to pay a price. It is never easy to make fundamental changes to our lives, and often those changes require us to sacrifice things (including relationships) that have grown dear to us. If you are confronted with a situation requiring a decision that bears a significant cost, it may be that you are confronting a Defining Moment. Those changes and sacrifices come in all shapes and sizes, but if we are walking in righteousness and listening to God, they are always worth it because God has a plan for our lives.[5]

A trip to Israel was a Defining Moment in Brad Howard's life that illustrates many of these principles.

After twenty years of being senior pastor at Lakeshore, Brad wanted to do something special, both as a vacation and to enhance his ministry.

After prayer and a lot of consideration, Brad and Denise decided to go on a trip to Israel with a group from Lakeshore Church that was being led by my wife, Mary, and me. Although Brad knew this had the potential to be a trip of a lifetime, there were definitely obstacles that he needed to overcome. For one, Brad hated to fly, and the trip would include flights of more than eight hours each way. Additionally, like many senior pastors, it was never easy to leave his church, and Brad would be away from the church for two weeks.

However, Brad was able to look beyond and overcome those stress points because in his heart he knew that this trip to Israel was going to be a Defining Moment in his life and in his ministry. He felt confirmation from the Holy Spirit that he and Denise were to go and that this was going to be a time of change for them. Brad's recognition that he was facing a life-changing moment allowed him to brush aside the anxieties he felt and move forward with the trip. By walking in righteousness, Brad heard from that Holy Spirit that he would be a different person and pastor after the trip.

What happened after that point of recognition and confirmation is amazing. It would have been easy for Brad to go on the trip in a "senior pastor" role, with confidence that based upon his training and experience, he knew all he needed for this pilgrimage to the Holy Land. However, the fact that he knew this trip was going to be special made him willing to jettison his preconceived notions of what Israel would be and head into the trip with a willingness and intention to be changed by it. Brad prepared by reading the day-by-day summaries of the trip that were provided in advance. He studied to have a better knowledge of each site they would see on the trip. Further, so he could focus totally on what God had for him to learn in Israel, Brad made it clear that he didn't want any leadership role on the trip. Brad knew that this would be a special time in his life before they left, and he wanted to get everything possible out of it.

That anticipation, preparation, and willingness to let God work in his life caused the trip to change him forever, both personally and in his ministry at Lakeshore Church. It was as if before the trip he read the Bible in black and white and now he read it in color! It has enabled him to preach and teach with a more personal understanding of what is contained in the Bible, and with a new enlightenment of the meaning of the stories used as a backdrop for his messages. The trip also greatly impacted his wife, Denise, and allowed her to minister more effectively at the church. As Denise put it, it's like she now has knowledge of the genealogy of her faith, similar to her knowledge of her family genealogy.

Brad's recognition that he was facing a Defining Moment allowed him to analyze it and understand the impact it could have on him. That, in turn, caused him to respond effectively through study and preparation and to absorb everything that they encountered on the trip. All of this allowed him to maximize the experience and his life was changed forever. This is what all of us are called to do—to maximize the impact of the opportunities God sets before us.

CHAPTER 3

Permanent Change

"Life is a matter of choices, and every choice you make makes you."

—JOHN MAXWELL

Sometimes it seems like we live in a world with no permanence, where "forever" is a myth or a romantic notion. Too often, we think that decisions we make are not permanent and can be changed without penalty. That perceived lack of permanence is itself a myth, often used to excuse away mistakes. In reality, each decision we make does impact and affect the remainder of our lives, almost like an individual's pay-it-forward *butterfly effect*[1]—only in this case the consequences affect the rest of our lives rather than the rest of the world.

Now let's clarify one thing right away: when we talk about permanence in this chapter, we're not going to focus on the "immaterial" decisions in life. Each of us make decisions every day, even some important decisions, that we do not intend and frankly do not want to be permanent. When you buy a car or a house, you probably don't expect that you will be driving it or living in it the rest of your life. Similarly, when you take that first real job, it can be a huge step for you with a significant impact upon the remainder of your life, but you don't expect it to last forever. While decisions like that can have an impact on the rest of your life (for example overspending and incurring too much debt), the decision itself is not intended to be a permanent decision. In this chapter we are going to focus on changes that are made to our character that will shape who we are ten, twenty, and thirty years from now, or even longer.

COMPOUNDING CHANGES

When we are talking about Defining Moments and their impact on our lives, we are by definition talking about changes to our essential character and the very nature of who we are. Those are changes we want to be permanent because we want them to shape us into being different than we were before. Therefore, it is important that those changes make us better. We want to make decisions that will change us and lead us down a path that will further refine our character and lead us to additional permanent changes. This idea of character change building upon prior character changes is almost like the financial concept of compounding interest, but with a deeper, more spiritual reward. The longer we keep improving our character through good decisions, the more refined our character becomes and the greater our reward of a full and rich life.

We are given a remarkably clear example of this in the classic Christian book, *Pilgrim's Progress.* At the beginning of the book, the main character, Christian, is standing outside his house dressed in rags with a book in his hand and a great burden upon his back. As he reads the book, he weeps and trembles and breaks out into a lamentable cry, saying, "What shall I do?" and later, "What shall I do to be saved?" As you read the book, you can feel the depth of his struggle and it is clear that Christian is facing a Defining Moment at this point in his life. As he struggles with this momentous decision, he is approached by a man named Evangelist. Evangelist makes Christian confront the enormity of his decision and points him in the direction of a shining light. Evangelist tells Christian to "keep that light in your eye, and go up directly thereto," and promises that he will find a gate where, upon knocking, Christian would be told what to do.

Upon being confronted with this decision and being told the way to eternal life, Christian begins to run. This becomes a Defining Moment in his life, as his character and purpose are changed forever. His wife and children cry after him to return, but he runs on and refuses to look behind. His neighbors also come out and try to stop him, but he continues like the man he became in the instant he made his decision, a man possessed by the dream of eternal life. As he moves along the road to heaven, Christian confronts many challenges, but he will not let anyone dissuade him. Christian was confronted with a Defining Moment in his life and made a decision to proceed forward. That decision brought about a permanent change in his life.

As we follow Christian through the allegory, we see him confronted by many other decision points—from characters he meets that try to turn him away, to places like Vanity Fair, where he is tempted by all that the world has to offer. Yet he never turns back from that permanent decision that he has made, because that decision, and that initial Defining Moment, changed him forever. All the later temptations and challenges he meets serve to further define and refine his character, but those later decisions do not turn him from that initial permanent change he made when confronted by Evangelist.

As we study the topic of Defining Moments, we need to remember that we should be driven by the same guiding principle. We are to make correct decisions with a goal of permanence in the development of our personhood. If we recognize, assess, and respond effectively to Defining Moments in our lives, each subsequent decision we make strengthens who we are as it further shapes, establishes, and refines our character and our inner being toward the goal of becoming all that we can be in Christ. As we go forward, we, like Christian, will build upon the foundation of the prior permanent changes that we have made. If we get offtrack—like Christian did when he chose the By-path Meadow rather than continuing on the Holy Way—we will need to retrace our steps. But we will be retracing our steps back to the place we were travelling when we were last on the right path. From there, we will continue forward, making future decisions based upon those prior, good, permanent decisions that we have previously made.

LONG-TERM SIGNIFICANCE OF CROSSROADS DECISIONS

Over forty years ago I experienced a distinct, Defining Moment when I decided to change from having a generally negative to a generally positive view of life. Consequently, I hesitate to focus on negative examples—but sometimes they illustrate a point very well, so from time to time we will use them in this book. This is especially true regarding the long-term impact of bad decisions made at Defining Moments in our lives.

I had a friend in college; we'll call him Jay for purposes of this book. Jay was a good guy and good student who had grown up in a very sheltered environment. His gift was writing, and you could see that in his activities at school—campus newspaper, yearbook, etc. He was diligent and contributed to making campus life better for his fellow students. You probably have known your own version of Jay.

College was a great experience for me, and I had great success there. However, I was at best a nominal, church-going Christian and wasn't really concerned about following the restrictive rules of the conservative Christian university I was attending. During my senior year I had my sights set for my next step and was ready to move on.

During that last year I ran into Jay one day on campus. He told me that he had never drunk a beer and asked if I would go out with him and have one (or two …). Always up for a little fun, and oblivious to what was going on at the moment, I gladly agreed to do so and we went out for the night. Jay had fun, I had fun, and that was about the end of it as far as I was concerned. I graduated from college, went to law school, got married, and pursued my career, not thinking any more about Jay or our night out.

Twenty years or so later, I got a letter from Jay and we reconnected briefly. He recounted to me that after that night, he drank more and more, and his life pretty much went into the ditch for years. Unfortunately, Jay struggled with alcohol addiction for years. Fortunately, however, he had recently turned his life around and had a job where he was able to pursue his passion of writing. However, the decision he made that night during our senior year had taken him down a path that cost him what should have been twenty of the most productive years of his life.

For now I will set aside the feelings of discouragement, despair, and depression I felt when I realized I had been part of a negative Defining Moment in Jay's life. We are each responsible for our own actions, but it seemed to me that I contributed to Jay's loss of twenty years of productive life. I obsessed about the impact my decisions that evening had on Jay's life. We will touch on that topic later in the book.

The point of the story is that on that night in 1977 Jay was at a crossroads in his life—a crossroads that became a Defining Moment for the next twenty years of his life. Jay likely didn't recognize it. Therefore, he didn't analyze the evening well, and certainly didn't respond effectively to the seemingly simple decision facing him that night. Unfortunately, he paid for that decision and his series of subsequent decisions for years. We are again shown the permanent impact on our lives of decisions we make.

We need to realize that when we are faced with Defining Moments, we are confronting decisions and opportunities that will affect us long into the future. That is why it is so important that we handle them properly. While we often (but certainly not always) have the ability to reverse course on bad decisions we have made, we need to understand that those decisions can stay with us and affect the course of our lives for a long, long time. Yet, remarkably, we often make those bad choices despite knowing better and despite being provided with better directions. In Jeremiah 6:16 (NLT), the Bible says: "This is what the LORD says: 'Stop at the crossroads and look around. Ask for the old, godly way, and walk in it. Travel its path, and you will find rest for your souls.' But you reply, 'No, that's not the road we want!'" We must get to a place where we are willing to accept biblical direction and follow the road God wants us to take, even if we want to take a different road.

The decisions made in those moments can take us down a road that changes the direction of our lives. Heading down a pathway in life is similar to driving down a highway. When you are driving north on U.S. 385 in Colorado and arrive at the intersection with Interstate 70, a left turn or a right turn determines whether you will drive into the Rocky Mountains or across hundreds of miles of wheat fields. Depending upon the route you take, your experiences and opportunities will be vastly different. Significantly, if you take the wrong turn, you will realize that the longer you drive the longer it takes you to get back to where you wanted to be. Wrong turns at Defining Moments are the same. Jay took a wrong turn, and the longer he went in that direction the further it took him from where he wanted to be, the longer it took him to get back to the point where he could start over, and the more time he had lost.

Bad responses to Defining Moments not only cause us to lose time, but they also cause us to see a completely different set of life opportunities. If you fail to properly deal with the Defining Moments in your life, you often won't be able to make the same choices you could have made to achieve your life dreams if you had handled those Defining Moments better. If you turn east on I-70, your options are much different than they would have been if you had turned west—options ranging from things as simple as entertainment availability to as significant as job opportunities. In the same way, your life options are affected by choices and decisions made if you fail to recognize, analyze, and respond effectively to the Defining Moments in your life.

When considering the importance of making good decisions it is important to remember how difficult it is to recover from bad decisions. It is never easy to change directions. We talked earlier about *negative inertia* and how we tend to keep moving in a direction because we get comfortable. (Remember Newton's first law of motion?) It is very important to remember this when discussing the long-term consequences of our decisions. If we don't handle Defining Moments well, we still need to deal with the consequences of the choices we make. Often what happens is that we adjust and get comfortable in the situation we are in—or even if we don't get *comfortable*, we at least learn how to deal with the situation. When that happens, negative inertia takes over and we can get stuck in a rut we never meant to walk into and stay there for years.

We have probably all known people that seem miserable in their vocations. I remember talking to a successful attorney like this early in my career. He was several years my senior, and we were working late one night to close a transaction. During a lull in our activity, he made a comment about how miserable he was, how he disliked the work he was doing, and that he never really wanted to pursue a legal career but did so because it was an easy course for him to follow. My naiveté was on full display when I asked him, quite simply, why he didn't do something else. He looked at me with a mixture of amazement and chagrin and quickly and succinctly pointed out that it wasn't that simple. His wife had expectations, they had a house with a big mortgage, his children liked to go skiing for spring break, etc. He was comfortable (or making due) in his life, but he also felt boxed in by earlier decisions he had made that had long-term consequences on his life and on his happiness.

Remember, decisions you make in the Defining Moments of your life can have long-term significance. In fact, they are often more permanent than you might think. It is therefore extremely important that you deal with those situations well and respond to them effectively with good decisions—your future depends on it!

SECOND CHANCES ARE OFTEN SECOND BEST

Years ago, Richard Roberts, the son of the famous evangelist Oral Roberts, wrote a book titled, *He's the God of a Second Chance*. Richard was an extremely talented singer and the heir apparent of both one of the most successful Christian ministries in the world and of the world-renowned university that bore his father's name. At the peak of his success, and at a time when divorce was not easily accepted in the Christian community, Richard and his wife, Patti, were divorced. In the book, Richard tells his story of going through that painful time, getting remarried, and coming to know that God is a God of second chances.

God's grace and the opportunity for second chances represent a biblical truism. From Adam through the apostles, we encounter story after story in the Bible that show how God's grace allows people to turn their lives around. The abundance of God's grace is illustrated in Matthew 18:21-22. We are told to forgive our brother not seven times, but seventy times seven times. Certainly if we are commanded to forgive so frequently, God must be willing to forgive us even more. That is good news.

However, while we all should rejoice in the fact that He is a God of second chances, we also need to realize that second chances are not as good as first chances! It is undeniable that if we are looking for a second chance, or a "do-over," it means that we failed, at least to some extent, in our first chance, and failure is never good. One way or another, we missed God's will for our lives and require another chance. That in and of itself is testimony that a second chance is not as good as success with the first chance.

But the occurrence of a failure is only one problem with needing a second chance. Oftentimes that initial failure, loss, or missed opportunity carries with it a burden or cross to bear that is difficult to overcome and that can keep us from becoming all that we can be in Christ. We might know that God has forgiven us, but the baggage of that prior failure may weigh us down for years. We can likely all point to examples of people who never were able to get on track after messing up their first opportunity. I have a dear friend and mentor who has spent years trying to overcome his lost first chance, only to see the baggage of the prior missed opportunity frustrate his subsequent efforts at success.

We also need to consider that second chances impact others in our lives. In a later chapter of this book, we will talk about the impact of our Defining Moments on other people. But in the context of discussing second chances, we need to consider the impact that missing God's perfect will (*a.k.a., first chances*) for our lives has on others. Each of us has a circle of friends, family, and close acquaintances that we influence. If we make the most of the Defining Moments God puts before us, we will experience His perfect will and the best that He has for us. If we are walking in His perfect will, we will be walking in a place of His blessing, and those blessings will impact others around us. Conversely, if we miss that opportunity, those around us will not participate in the impact of that blessing on their lives. We need to be grateful if we are given a second chance, but unfortunately, it is likely that our opportunities from those second chances will not impact the world and those around us to the same extent as if we had acted on the first chances God gave us.

The Bible makes it clear that God has a perfect will for each of us.[2] If we fail to follow His plan, if we miss the opportunities God presents to us in those Defining Moments that we encounter, God will seek after someone else to do the work and receive the blessing that was intended for us.[3] In addition to each of us missing our blessing from missing God's will, we can only wonder who in our circle of acquaintances would have missed the blessings that we could have brought their way, and whether the same work for God's Kingdom will be accomplished by the others that have had to pick up the mantle that God had prepared for us.

Kathryn Kuhlman, a Spirit-filled female evangelist of the twentieth century, said many times that she did not believe she was God's first choice for the ministry she had. Rather, she believed that God had called some man to do the work that He did through her ministry, but that man, whoever he was, was unwilling to pay the price. While we can look at Ms. Kuhlman and call her ministry a great success, we must acknowledge that if she was correct in her analysis, someone else was intended for that role. That person's failure to seize upon the opportunities presented to him had multiple consequences. First, it relegated him to second best for his life. Additionally, it kept others in his circle of acquaintances from realizing the blessings they would have experienced through his ministry, had he pursued it. Finally, as dynamic as Ms. Kuhlman's ministry was, the ministry of God's intended person would have been different, and therefore, the ministry God intended for him may have been at least partially unfulfilled.

WHEN PERMANENT CHANGE BECOMES SHORT TERM

So we see that Defining Moments should lead us to places where we are permanently changed, that those changes compound upon one another, and that God is gracious enough to give us second chances. That all sounds good, especially the grace part. However, we cannot overemphasize the importance of consistently *recognizing, analyzing,* and *responding effectively* to Defining Moments in our lives. God put us on earth for a purpose, and becoming all that He wants us to be typically takes time, often a lifetime, and even then we don't seem to quite get to that place of being perfect as our Father in heaven is perfect.[4]

Our lives on earth are finite, which means that we have limited time to accomplish the work God has set before us. In fact, the Bible tells us to number our days, so that we may apply our hearts to wisdom.[5] The longer it takes us to get on the proper path, the more Defining Moments we miss, the less time we have to fulfill His purposes. In effect, the *permanence* of the change we achieve is still there; it's just that *permanent* becomes *short term*—at least it is here on earth.[6]

It seems so obvious, but yet it is an essential point. The longer we wait to begin taking advantage of the opportunities presented in our Defining Moments, the less time we have for the changes that come with them to accomplish good works and spiritual development. The sooner we begin the process of perfecting ourselves in Him, the longer we have to accomplish His purpose for us on earth, and the more of an impact we can have on the world around us. The finite nature of our lives necessarily means that the changes brought about by the second chances God gives to us are never as efficacious as the changes that could have been made by good use of the first chances we had.

One of the saddest life stories in the Bible is the story of Samson, as told in chapters 13-16 of the book of Judges. It is a story of both amazing unrealized potential, and a very short-term second chance. For some reason we don't understand, God chose to raise up a superhero, and because of that it remains one of the most exciting stories ever told.

Before Samson was born, his potential was evidenced by the fact that an angel appeared to his mother to announce his birth. This puts him in pretty rare company, since the only other people whose births were the subject of angelic preannouncements in the Bible were Isaac, John the Baptist, and Jesus Christ. We certainly do not know why God sent an angel to tell Samson's mother about her son's birth, but with all things considered, it leads us to the conclusion that God intended Samson for greatness. His potential is also evident from the superhuman strength that was given to him. Samson was to be dedicated as a Nazirite to God from the womb to the day of his death and was chosen to be a judge of Israel in the time period before kings, but neither of these things were an experience unique to Samson. However, there is no one else in the Bible that was given the physical strength of Samson. He was special!

Despite all of his potential, Samson chose to squander it by living a licentious, hedonistic life. The story of his relationship with Delilah is one of the most famous stories in Western civilization and has been addressed in books, movies, and songs. Yet his life veered off course long before he knew Delilah. Time after time he violated the Nazirite vows that he was sworn to. To put it in the context of our discussion, he was presented with multiple opportunities for Defining Moments and yet never seemed to make good decisions in those moments. He chose to rely upon the superhuman strength God had given him rather than to develop his character to use that strength to judge the nation of Israel wisely and to deliver Israel from the Philistines as God intended for him to do. He routinely failed to recognize the moments, assess and evaluate them well, or to respond effectively. He had a lot of great experiences, but those experiences didn't change who he was.

However, while serving as a slave to the Philistines after his fall, Samson had time to realize the error of his ways. He asked God for a second chance. This time when God answered his prayer, Samson took advantage of his second chance and used it to bring destruction to the Philistines. Unfortunately, that event also resulted in his death. However, even that story highlights the tragedy of Samson's life. We can only wonder what victorious stories would have resulted had he utilized the Defining Moments presented to him earlier in his life to become the man that God intended him to be. We can clearly see, however, that because he missed those opportunities he was not able to develop the character necessary to fulfill the potential of the angelic announcement of his birth. He never became the great judge of Israel that would deliver his people from the bondage of the Philistines.

Samson's life serves as an example of the famous quote attributed to Texas football coach Darrell Royal: "Potential just means you ain't done it yet." God gives each of us great potential. We need to seize the opportunities presented in the Defining Moments we face and fulfill our potential. We need to *do it*.

CHAPTER 4

Nuts and Bolts

"The putter looks like a bunch of nuts and bolts welded together, but the ball goes in the hole."

—Julius Boros[1]

I think that somewhere deep down inside, most guys want to be or maybe even think they are a good mechanic; not necessarily as a career, but just to be good enough to know that if something is broken, we can fix it. I'm not sure why that is. Maybe it's a need to be self-reliant, to think that we can fix our own problems—car problems or equipment around the house. Maybe it has something to do with a basic love for cars and trucks, and a desire to build, repair, or restore something that is bigger, faster, and better looking than we are—something that we can show off.

Growing up on a farm in the sixties, it wasn't just cool to be a mechanic, it was necessary. My father, who also grew up on a farm but was educated and licensed as an Assemblies of God minister, could seemingly fix anything. If a tractor broke, he could fix it. If a car or truck quit running, he was quick to open the hood or crawl under the vehicle, diagnose the problem, and know what part was needed. He then was able to install the part, reassemble the vehicle, and restart it. Amazing!

Inspired by our father on the farm, my brother and I thought we could be mechanics also. Dad had an old John Deere Model M tractor that even he had given up on, but we thought we could get it running and then either sell it for a profit or use it in our own future farming operations. Not wanting to discourage our entrepreneurial spirit, Dad gave us permission to work on the tractor. We spent the better part of one summer disassembling that old tractor in an attempt to figure out why it wouldn't run. In the end we realized that not only could we not diagnose the problem, *but we also were not able to put the tractor back together!* That was the beginning of my realization that I needed to pursue a career other than being a mechanic.

Like a good mechanic we need good problem-solving skills to maximize the positive consequences of Defining Moments in our lives. These skills center around recognition, analysis, and evaluation, and then effective responses to Defining Moments in our lives. Our responses to Defining Moments are the culmination of a process in which each of these steps is integrated with the other steps. You must *recognize* before you *analyze* and *evaluate*, and without *analyzing* and *evaluating* the situation, it is unlikely that you will *respond effectively*.

Like all life skills, these abilities are developed and improved over time, but we must start with identifying what they are. In this chapter we will address some of the nuts and bolts of dealing with Defining Moments.

RECOGNIZING THE OBVIOUS

If you are at a point in your life that has the potential to change the essential character of who you are or the direction that your life will take, it should be obvious, right? You would think so, but that is not always the case. Sometimes we just flat out miss the moments. That doesn't mean that the Defining Moments we miss won't impact us; just that we may miss the opportunities that go with them. Therefore, the challenge before us is to recognize those moments and maximize their positive impact upon us.

There are many reasons for failing to recognize that we are facing a Defining Moment. One reason for missing these moments is the negative inertia we have discussed previously. As we grow comfortable in our day-to-day lives, it is easy to continue travelling in our individual ruts, especially when there is nothing pushing us to change. The comfort and normalcy of our routines can easily prevent us from even seeing that we are approaching a milestone in the road; and the deeper you are in your individual rut, the harder it is to peek over the edge and look outside of it to see the opportunities available to you.

Sometimes we also fail to recognize Defining Moments because we are looking for "big things" and do not realize that Defining Moments can arrive at what may appear to be insignificant moments in our lives. I doubt that most people would consider an eleven-year-old boy spending his money at a travelling carnival show to be a significant moment. However, if that eleven-year-old boy makes a vow to never do that again and then sticks with it the remainder of his life, that seemingly insignificant moment can become a Defining Moment that will change the course of his life and his financial future. This principle is also borne out in Scripture. In 1 Kings 19, the prophet Elijah is despairing of his life and looking for a word from God. The Bible says that the Lord was not in the strong wind, the earthquake, or the fire, but was in a still, small voice. We need to be aware that even small, apparently insignificant things can set the stage for Defining Moments in our lives.

Additionally, we can miss the significance of Defining Moments because we are not living the lives that we should be living. If we took a wrong turn previously, we will have different opportunities than those that would face us had we been travelling in the right direction. Similarly, if we are not living our lives according to the proper principles and practices, we may not be tuned in to the proper spiritual frequencies that would allow us to recognize the moments facing us. In this regard, it is vitally important that we live our lives in a way that prepares us to maximize the opportunities arising from the Defining Moments in our lives.

A clear example of the consequences of missing a Defining Moment is the story of Orpah in the first chapter of the book of Ruth. Naomi and her husband had travelled from the land of Israel to the land of Moab to flee a famine. While in Moab, Naomi's husband died, and her two sons were married to women from that land, Orpah and Ruth. Naomi's hard times continued when her two sons died. At that point she told her two daughters-in-law that they should abandon her and go back to their mothers' homes. Naomi explained that they would have better chances in life by staying in their homeland than by travelling back to Israel with her. Naomi was telling them to move on with their lives.

At this point, the Bible says Orpah kissed her mother-in-law and went back to her people and her gods. In other words, she continued in the life she had always lived and did not recognize the Defining Moment and the opportunities that she was facing. The Bible does not tell us why Orpah turned from Naomi, just that she did. Maybe it was because Orpah was stuck in a rut and couldn't see out of it, or maybe it was because she was looking for something more important than staying with a woman (Naomi) who seemed to have nothing but bad luck. Whatever the reason, Orpah chose to separate from Naomi and disappears from the biblical record. While we will never know what would have been in store for Orpah had she gone to the land of Israel, we can see what happened to her sister-in-law, Ruth, and justifiably imagine that Orpah missed out on blessings God had in store for her. As we know, Ruth went to Israel, met and married a wealthy man named Boaz, and went on to give birth to Obed, thereby becoming the great-great-grandmother of King David and ultimately in the lineage of Christ. Orpah, on the other hand, disappeared from recorded history.

It's a shame to miss a Defining Moment in our lives and the opportunities that go with it. We need to be on the lookout for them, but what should we be looking for? There are many things that can help us recognize these critical points in our lives, but here are a few obvious indicators:

1. *Are you at a crossroads?* Defining Moments shape our essential character. Often we encounter these moments when we are faced with major decisions, especially in our personal lives. Things like changing careers, relocating, marriage, or having children will certainly change the direction of your life, and the decisions made in those times can also reveal and shape your essential character. When you are at a crossroads point in your life, focus on the decisions you are making, as they may change you forever.

2. *Are you in a crisis situation?* You can be at a crossroads without being in crisis, and you can be in a crisis without being at a crossroads. When your life is in crisis, decisions seem to be more difficult and take on greater significance. More importantly, when you are in those crisis times you often feel pressured to compromise your character. When your character is tested, your *essential* character can be shaped, and those are the times that define who you really are.

3. *Will your decision impact others?* When confronted with a Defining Moment in your life, it is very likely that the decisions you make will affect others. In fact, the greater the impact your decision has on others, the more likely the issue you are facing is a Defining Moment. This is because those decisions reveal if we are willing to set aside our goals and personal interests to help others. Our choices in those moments can reveal the extent of our selfishness, and good choices are often selfless ones that shape our essential character.

While Orpah may have missed a Defining Moment in her life, her sister-in-law, Ruth, recognized the moment and realized maximum benefits as a result. By applying the tests above, it is easy to recognize that Ruth was facing a Defining Moment. Their family was clearly at a crossroads, as her mother-in-law, Naomi, was planning to move back to the land of Judah. Ruth was clearly in a time of crisis, with the recent death of both her husband and father-in-law. Finally, her decision would impact others, in this case Naomi, the person she was then closest to. Because Ruth recognized that she was facing a Defining Moment in her life, she was able to properly analyze the situation and respond in a way that changed her life forever, and for the better.

ANALYSIS RELIEVES PARALYSIS

A person confronted by a major decision may suffer from *paralysis by analysis.* This describes a situation where a person cannot make a decision because they spend too much time analyzing it and are frozen in indecision. This can be crippling and may result in missing great opportunities.

However, just as common and just as damaging is to suffer from *paralysis by lack of analysis.* I have seen many situations where a person is unable to make a major decision (and certainly unable to make a *good* decision) because they have not adequately analyzed the situation. In fact, I believe that in most cases proper analysis and evaluation will provide the wisdom necessary to allow a person to make a good decision.

If you recognize that you are at a Defining Moment, you should realize that what you do at that moment has the possibility of changing your life and your future forever. As you stand at that precipice of decision, it is important to analyze the situation, but it is equally important to acknowledge that you must make a decision based upon that analysis. In these situations it is critical to remember the biblical command to get wisdom, for it will protect you.[2]

Let's look at the steps we can to take in this process of evaluating and analyzing Defining Moments.

1. *What decision must I make?* This seems an obvious question, but it is amazing how often people don't focus on the issue at hand. It is common to clutter up your decision with issues collateral or even sometimes unrelated to the issue at hand, and this always makes it more difficult to make a good decision. When you are at a moment of decision, focus on the specific decision that needs to be made, not collateral issues, and it is much easier to reach a conclusion.

2. *Get the facts.* You cannot make a good decision if you fail to consider the relevant facts. However, people often fail to expend the time and energy necessary to determine the facts, or they do not want to consider them because the facts may represent things they do not want to acknowledge. When you are buying a piece of property, it is important that you do the necessary due diligence to understand what you are buying. The same thing is true with any decision you make. Learn the facts, and you will make a better decision.

3. *Analyze the consequences.* When you are facing a Defining Moment in your life, you are at a crossroads point. In those situations, it is important that you analyze the consequences of all possible choices. If your decision takes you closer to achieving your life goals and objectives, and if it takes you on the path that God has planned for you, then you are probably making the correct decision. Alternatively, if your decision unnecessarily defers achieving your life goals and objectives, or results in consequences inconsistent with God's will for your life, most likely it is a bad decision. Again, this sounds so simple, but it is so common for people to ignore evaluating the consequences of their decisions before making them. This often leads to negative outcomes.

After going through these steps, you should have a clear picture of all the issues involved with the Defining Moment facing you. At that point, you have all the information necessary to make a good decision—so you can make and implement that decision with confidence!

RESPONDING WITH CHARACTER

It seems that if you recognized a Defining Moment and analyzed it properly, you would certainly make the best decision possible. However, that is not always the case. In fact, as we saw previously in the story of the rich young ruler, sometimes when facing the most significant decisions in our lives we willfully make choices that are wrong and which send us completely in the wrong direction. However, the *recognition, analysis,* and *evaluation* are all wasted if the *response* is incorrect.

Making sound decisions is not always easy, but there are some steps we can take to improve the likelihood of making the best possible responses when confronted with Defining Moments. Here are a few of those steps:

1. *Identify the Options.* Identifying the available options is closely related to the analysis phase, but different. In the analysis phase, we narrowed the question to be answered; in the response phase we should identify all of the possible choices that can be made to answer that question. I recently had a friend who was trying to sell a property that would have resulted in a significant profit to him. He thought he had reached agreement on the transaction, but the deal began to fall apart over the payment terms—which is not an insignificant issue. My friend was so focused on the profit to be made that payment seemed to be only a yes or no decision. After we spoke with the purchaser, I suggested an alternative payment structure, with security for payment of the price during a contingency period. This was acceptable to both parties and the transaction was able to close. By expanding the field of

available options and not just looking at a single yes or no option, we were able to accomplish both parties' objectives.

2. *Respond in a Manner Consistent with Biblical Principles.* We live in a world where too often people are told to make decisions based upon what feels right. While that sounds nice, it is a terrible decision-making strategy. As Christians, we look to the Bible as a source of wisdom. Even though the Bible may not provide direct and specific answers for every question we face in life, it does provide a standard for determining right from wrong and life principles to guide us in making good decisions. For example, the Bible won't tell you whether or not you should marry a specific person, but it will set forth principles (like not being unequally yoked or not living with a contentious spouse) which will allow you to make a good decision. You cannot expect God to bless your decisions if those decisions are contrary to biblical principles.

3. *Plan Ahead for Your Defining Moments.* In many ways, this is a corollary to making decisions based upon biblical principles. You should think about situations that you may have to deal with in the future and consider how you will respond to them—and those responses should be based upon biblical principles. This will prepare you for future crisis situations that otherwise might catch you by surprise. In my forty years of practicing law, I have seen many people get into financial, legal, ethical, and other problems, oftentimes with severe, and sometimes criminal, consequences. However, rarely have I seen that happen without the seeds of those bad decisions being planted in advance. Typically, bad decisions which result in serious consequences begin with prior, less significant decisions that change a person's character to the point where he or she is comfortable making those bad decisions. Conversely, if you decide in advance to do the right thing and live consistent with biblical principles, then

even in small moments you will avoid making bad decisions with possibly disastrous consequences.

———————

Rahab, a non-Israelite, is one of the most interesting characters in the story of the exodus of the children of Israel from Egypt to the Promised Land. Her story first appears in the second and sixth chapters of the book of Joshua, it is continued in the first chapter of the book of Matthew, and it is prominently recounted in the eleventh chapter of the book of Hebrews. Few women in the Bible receive so much attention. Rahab was a harlot and for that reason an unlikely heroine; however, she seized upon her singular Defining Moment and changed the trajectory of her life.

When Rahab is introduced in the Bible, the Israelites had finished their forty-year trek in the wilderness, Moses had died, and Joshua was about to lead the people into the Promised Land. Prior to going over, Joshua sent two men as spies to determine what they would be facing. Those men went to the city of Jericho and stayed with Rahab, who hid them from the king and then helped them to escape. The men returned to Israel safely and advised Joshua that the Promised Land was theirs for the taking. Joshua led the people across the Jordan and they proceeded to conquer the land. Let's take a look at how Rahab's reaction to this Defining Moment in her life changed her forever.

First, Rahab *recognized* that she was facing a Defining Moment in her life. She and all the people in Jericho knew the Israelites were approaching and that God had provided them great success—from crossing the Red Sea as they came out of Egypt to victories over the Amorites during their wilderness journey. In Joshua 2, Rahab also says that the people of Jericho were in fear and believed that because God was with the Israelites, the city of Jericho had no chance of withstanding them. Rahab saw that (1) she was in a crisis situation—an attack from Israel would have devastating consequences to Jericho and her; (2) she was at a crossroads—she could continue as she was living or she could stand with the God of the Israelites; and (3) the situation she faced could impact her family—as they were facing the same risks as the rest of Jericho.

After *recognizing* this Defining Moment, Rahab *analyzed* and *evaluated* the situation. She understood the decision to be made and was able to analyze the consequences—she could either turn in the two spies and continue in her existing life, hoping the attack would never come, or she could help them escape and save herself and her family. Rahab evaluated this decision and its consequences in light of the critical facts that she knew—that the Israelites were led by God, who had helped them to win the prior battles they had faced.

As we noted previously, facing a Defining Moment is a cumulative process, from *recognition* to *analysis to responding effectively.* When we look at the story of Rahab in that light, it is easy to see the best decision and response for her to make—to choose the side of God, and trust in Him. That is what she did by hiding the two spies, pleading for mercy for herself and her family, helping the spies escape, and then following their instructions to bind the scarlet cord to her window and keep her family in her house when the attack occurred.

Rahab's recognition, analysis, and response to this Defining Moment in her life forever changed the trajectory of her life. When the Israelites attacked later, the two spies went into the city and took her and her family outside and saved their lives. While we are not told much more about Rahab's life, it is probably safe to assume that she no longer continued as a harlot. The Bible tells us that she was the mother of Boaz, who the Bible says was a man of great wealth.[3] As a result, she became the mother-in-law of Ruth and an ancestor of Christ. In fact, Rahab is only one of five women mentioned in Matthew's genealogy of Christ, and her response to her Defining Moment was so significant that it is noted in the *Hall of Faith* in chapter 11 of the book of Hebrews—where it is noted that Rahab did not perish with those who did not believe, but survived because she had received the spies with peace.[4]

Certainly, Rahab never foresaw all of this when she made her decision to trust in God and help the two spies. However, her story shows us that even though we may not know all the consequences of our actions when we are facing Defining Moments, we can expect that they will have long-term and even eternal consequences for not only each of us as we face those moments, but also for generations to follow.

CHAPTER 5

Some Moments Matter More

"A life totally committed to God has nothing to fear,
nothing to lose, nothing to regret."

—Pandita Ramabai

Brad and I had very different conversion experiences.

Lorne: My father was educated and trained as a minister, and I grew up in a family where three church services a week and Sunday school were the norm, and family devotions before bedtime happened more often than not. I made a childhood profession of faith in Christ at age eight during a week-long evangelistic crusade conducted by the Reverend Harold May. However, that decision did not result in a massive life change, and, in reality, I probably viewed it more as "fire insurance" than anything else. I lived my life as a "cultural Christian" (which was much easier in the 60s and 70s than it is today), and went through college and on to law school without having a real, life-changing, Defining Moment in my spiritual life. That moment came at the end of the most spiritually challenging year of my life. I made a firm, never-looking-back commitment to Christ in November, 1978, in South Bend, Indiana, when Mary and I were confronted with the evil of the Jonestown massacre. We were watching a television interview with one of Mary's childhood friends who had been a part of the Jim Jones *Peoples Temple* cult, but had not gone to British Guyana with them. That night, the Lord showed me with abundant clarity that evil was real, and that I was at a crossroads in my life. I needed to either truly repent and walk a Christian life, or continue down a pathway that would only lead me to a life further separated from God. I chose repentance.

Brad: I did not grow up in church. My family spent weekends at the lake with our grandparents, or most often, going our own separate ways. My introduction to Christ came through a high school biology teacher who reached out to me following the disappearance of my father. I would later find out why he left us, but at the time nothing could explain the deep sense of loss that gripped me in his absence. It was hard to breathe much less attend classes, and it was on one of those dark days that I couldn't get out of bed that Mr. Peek, my biology teacher, came knocking at my door. He wasn't there to condemn me for skipping school but to lead me to Christ. It would be some time later in the privacy of my bedroom that I would commit my life to Christ and have a powerful Defining Moment with God. I was sixteen at the time and knew I had received a divine calling to serve God in a significant way. Alan Peek, my teacher-turned-substitute father, continued to be there for me. During my senior year he opened his classroom for me to lead a weekly Bible study on our high school campus and somehow found the money to send me to Bible school. He continues to be an integral part of my life to this day. For me, it was a divine connection that led to the greatest Defining Moment of my life.

Despite these different experiences, both of us have made the decision to accept Christ as the Lord of our lives, and without question, the decision to commit your life to Christ, or not, is a Defining Moment in the life of every person who confronts it. While that is the most important spiritual decision that any of us will make, it is one of a series of spiritual

Defining Moments that we will face in our lives. However, because of the eternal impact of that decision and the vast character changes that result from adopting a biblical philosophy and lifestyle, our spiritual Defining Moments will impact us more than the personal and professional Defining Moments that we will discuss in the next two chapters.

Our spiritual journey can be seen as a continuous quest, with decisions and choices made daily that will impact our essential character. There are many spiritual decisions that serve to define who we are, but in this chapter we will focus on three specific decisions that we all face along the highway to heaven. All three of these decisions involve making a commitment. That's not surprising, because making commitments will change us. With that in mind, let's focus on the Defining Moments that matter more: our commitments to Christ, to discipleship, and to a community of believers.

COMMITMENT TO CHRIST

The decision to commit your life to Christ is the single most important Defining Moment in your life. From that moment on, your life shifts (or doesn't shift, depending upon the decision you make) to a new trajectory, a trajectory the leads to eternal life with God rather than eternal separation from God! However, making a commitment to Christ should also lead to significant changes in our outlook, attitudes, priorities, and behavior here on earth.

It is important that we define what we mean by a "Commitment to Christ." Unfortunately, even in our Christian churches there is no agreement on exactly what this means. We use many terms that seem to be referring to the same thing. Terms like "getting saved," "being converted," "becoming a Christ follower," "born again," "becoming a believer," "accepting Christ," and "being justified" are all included in the Christian lexicon. If this plethora of terminology is confusing even to those who are in the church, think how much more confusing it must be to people we are trying to reach.

For purposes of this book, we are referring to a *Commitment to Christ* as being the point in your life where you make a specific decision that you believe that Jesus Christ is the Son of God, acknowledge that you are a sinner and repent of your sins, accept the salvation that comes from Christ's sacrifice of His life, and commit your life to living according to godly, biblical teachings. Those are a lot of concepts to tie together in a single decision, which is why it may take more than a single encounter, discussion, sermon, etc., for someone to make a Commitment to Christ. The inclusion of all those concepts also emphasizes why it is so important that Christians do not fail to share the full message of conversion/salvation when talking with non-Christians. We should never make the act of becoming a Christian overly complicated, because it isn't. However, at the same time we shouldn't make it so casual that the person we are sharing with doesn't understand that they are being called to a total change of direction.

It is important to emphasize that a Commitment to Christ involves a specific decision, *i.e.*, a Defining Moment. In the book of John, Jesus told Nicodemus, a member of the Jewish ruling council, that no one can see the Kingdom of God unless he is "born again." Jesus went on to say that He was talking about a spiritual birth. Just as you became a child of your earthly parents when you were born physically, so you will become a child of God when you are born again spiritually. However, it is up to each of us to make that decision, and it is not optional. The Bible says that if you want to enter into the Kingdom of heaven, you *must* be born again. If we make that commitment, the Bible tells us that we are changed forever.[1]

After we have made a Commitment to Christ, we will continue to be confronted with choices requiring us to be faithful to our Commitment to Christ. The Bible tells us that even the most significant evangelist of all time, the apostle Paul, struggled with sin.[2] However, our Commitment to Christ should be evident in our lives. In his book, *Peace With God*, Billy Graham says that we should see five changes in our lives after we have been born again: (1) a different attitude toward sin; (2) a desire to obey God; (3) separation from the world; (4) a new love in our hearts for other people; and (5) we should not practice sin.[3] If we see all of those changes in our lives, it is evidence that our essential character is changing, and we can be confident that we have responded effectively to the most significant Defining Moment in our life.

At the beginning of this chapter we told two very different stories of salvation—of making a Commitment to Christ, and there are innumerable other, different salvation stories. The important thing is not *how* it happens, but *that* it happens. If you are reading this book and have not yet made a decision to commit your life to Christ, please do it today, wherever you may be. If you have questions, reach out to a church pastor or a Christian friend and ask them about this decision. Your essential character will be changed, for now and for eternity!

COMMITMENT TO DISCIPLESHIP

So we see that making a Commitment to Christ is a significant Defining Moment, but then what? Your initial conversion is only the first step, but you have the rest of your life ahead of you—now what are you supposed to do? As Christians, we must understand that our initial Commitment to Christ is not the end of our spiritual journey here on earth. Rather, it is just the beginning. There is so much more than that to the Christian life.

In his book, *After You Believe,* N. T. Wright addresses the important question of what happens after our Commitment to Christ. He points out that we should be encouraged and excited by the pursuit of virtue in its specifically Christian form, and to have our character shaped to become the human beings God meant us to be.[4] To discover what we are to become requires a paradigm shift, an acknowledgement that our conversion did not complete us and that we need to take affirmative steps to become what God wants us to be in this life on earth. It's what the apostle Paul was emphasizing to the Colossian church, "He is the one we proclaim, admonishing and teaching everyone with all wisdom, so that we may present everyone fully mature in Christ. To this end I strenuously contend with all the energy Christ so powerfully works in me."[5] Making the decision to become fully mature in Christ is what we refer to as the Commitment to Discipleship.

Making the decision to follow through and become a mature Christian is a Defining Moment in each of our lives and will result in the ongoing transformation of our essential character. However, the nature of this Defining Moment is that it leads to a *refining process*. It is necessary that it becomes more than a *moment*. A moment can be affected by emotion, but committing to the process takes discipline and that is what will change us. When Mary and I made our ultimate Commitment to Christ in 1978, we were certainly affected by the emotion of the *moment*. After that decision, we still had a lot of things that we needed to work through in our lives, and we were only able to work through those issues because we made a commitment to the *process* of discipleship.

At one point in His ministry on earth, Jesus told the crowd surrounding Him that, "Whoever wants to be my disciple must deny themselves and take up their cross and follow me."[6] Discipleship implies a close relationship to Christ, which should be the goal of every Christian. Developing that relationship and becoming disciples of Christ will change our essential character. Michael J. Wilkins, in a succinct discussion of discipleship, points this out by stating that there are three goals of discipleship: (1) to ourselves, the goal is to become like Christ; (2) to others, our goal is servanthood; and (3) to the world, our goal is to fulfill the Great Commission.[7] Character changes like that don't come automatically. Let's consider how we get there.

When a person makes a Commitment to Christ, he or she is saying that they repent from their sins and vow to move forward in a different direction. At the risk of oversimplifying, it's kind of like you have joined a team. Team membership is great, but you don't join a team just for the jersey. You join a team because you want to play and you want to be successful and contribute to the team's success. In order to do that, you have to study the playbook, be willing to be coached, and to practice regularly.

That's where discipleship comes in. It's kind of like the Bible is the playbook, the Holy Spirit is our coach, and practice involves prayer, church attendance, Bible studies, changing our habits, service to the body of Christ and our communities, and many other things that help make us disciples of Christ and thereby shape our character into the people that God intends for us to be. Prior to our Commitment to Christ, we probably did not even know what was involved in being a Christian, and we almost certainly weren't regularly engaged in the activities necessary to become a successful Christian team player. Therefore, new Christians need to make a specific commitment to discipleship (to become a new person in Christ), and that decision will be another Defining Moment in the lives of those who make it.

One of the clearest decisions to Commit to Discipleship is Christ calling His first disciples. The event is described in Matthew chapter 4. By this time, Jesus had been baptized by John the Baptist, finished forty days of fasting, experienced temptation by the devil, and was just beginning His public ministry. In Matthew 4:18-22, the Bible describes Jesus walking along the Sea of Galilee when He saw Simon Peter and his brother Andrew, who were fishermen. Jesus invited them to follow Him and become fishers of men, at which point they left their nets and followed Him. Continuing His walk, Jesus saw James and John, who were fishing in a boat with their father, and when He called to them, they also immediately left their boat and their father and followed Jesus. These four men spent the next two years being discipled by Jesus, which prepared them for establishing the early church and ultimately the beginning of the Christian faith.

Another great biblical example of the Commitment to Discipleship is in the second chapter of the book of Acts, where the beginning of the early church is described. At the beginning of the chapter, it describes how the Holy Spirit (our coach) came as a mighty rushing wind on the day of Pentecost and filled the followers of Christ who were gathered together. After being filled with the Holy Spirit, Peter spoke unto the people who were present in Jerusalem, telling them about the ministry, crucifixion, resurrection, and ascension of Christ into heaven. The Bible tells us that Peter's message was gladly received, and that on that day three thousand people were added to the church (joined the team). From there the story goes on, and we are told that after their conversion, these people continued steadfastly in the apostles' doctrine and fellowship and in sharing meals and in prayer (they practiced). In other words, they made a *Commitment to Discipleship*!

If Peter, Andrew, James and John, and the new converts on the day of Pentecost all made the decision to change their lives through discipleship, why would we think that we are not required to make a similar decision?

My decision to Commit to Discipleship (and to stay with it) is not nearly as dramatic as those biblical examples described above, but it certainly was a Defining Moment for me. I had finished law school and begun practicing law in Dallas. Mary and I had our first child and had begun attending Church on the Rock in Rockwall, Texas, which was founded and pastored at that time by Dr. Larry Lea. Larry is one of the most gifted preachers that I have ever heard, and our church was growing rapidly. Not long after we had joined the church, Larry preached a sermon series called "Could You Not Tarry One Hour?" which was intended to call believers to a more consistent prayer life centered on praying through the Lord's Prayer, which as Larry would frequently remind us is how Jesus told us we should pray.[8]

That message seemed so simple and yet it was a clarion call to me. During the prior years of my Christian life I had never had a consistent or meaningful prayer life, but now I had a method for praying that made perfect sense and I decided to grab on to it. At that time, Church on the Rock was having prayer services five days a week at 5:00 a.m., and I decided that I would attend those prayer services for at least six weeks to develop a habit of prayer. Each morning I would drag myself out of bed and try to leave our house by 4:30 a.m. That six-week commitment lasted for over a year and soon I was volunteering to work with Pastor Lea's prayer ministry and travelling with him to Prayer Breakthrough events.

In reality, although I thought that I was just making a six-week commitment to pray, I was actually making a *Commitment to Discipleship* and my life changed from that point forward. Mary and I became much more consistent in having regular family devotions with our children, I became much more committed to reading the Bible (and soon thereafter began reading through the Bible every year, which I continue to this day) and church attendance, and my life began to change in many ways. Although I no longer attend Church on the Rock, I can point to that commitment to prayer as one of the most significant Defining Moments of my life because at that point my character began to change. Those changes continue to the present, and even now when I pray, I use the Lord's Prayer as my guide.

COMMITMENT TO CHRISTIAN COMMUNITY

Considering all the money, time, and effort that is poured into churches in the United States, it is amazing that we so often miss the target of building a community of believers. It seems that modern American Christian culture has mastered the art of constructing buildings and operating institutions but is missing the point that we are supposed to be living in a community of believers where we bear one another's burdens and so fulfill the law of Christ.[9] It is important to note that building a true community of believers is much different than forming a Christian country club!

Your decision to choose and commit your life to a community of believers is a Defining Moment that can shape your character and through which you can have an impact on and help shape the character of others. To continue our earlier analogy, the decision to commit to a Christian community is kind of like the decision to play a team sport rather than golf or tennis.

The Bible has many passages that describe the importance of living together in a Christian community. One passage that is frequently quoted to remind us of the importance of attending church tells us that we should not forsake the assembling of ourselves together.[10] However, it is important to note that verse is the second portion of a sentence that begins with "[a]nd let us consider how we may spur one another on toward love and good deeds...."[11] By this, the Scripture is saying that the purpose of gathering together as a body of believers is to support other believers and to help each of us fulfill God's purposes for our lives. Unfortunately, too often in our Christian culture that verse is implicitly translated into meaning that Sunday morning church services are enough. In fact, building a strong Christian community takes much more than that—it requires developing a network of relationships which allow us to rely upon each other.

It is important to remember that there never has been and until Christ returns there never will be a perfect utopian society. However, as Christians we should work toward a stronger sense of community than what we generally experience today, and the Bible gives us examples. In the second chapter of the book of Acts, there are some general references to communal living involving the early church that we should consider. Those verses state that all who believed "were together, and had all things common," and that they continued "daily with one accord in the temple, and breaking bread from house to house...."

All that sounds great, but those passages also include verses which tend to frighten modern American Christians, saying that they "had all things common, and sold their possessions and goods, and parted them to all men, as every man had need."[12] That communal life is definitely not our culture. However, before making a decision to completely ignore these verses, it is important to note a couple points. First, there is not a biblical commandment that required the early church to live in this fashion. In fact, in the verses describing the actions and death of Ananias and Sapphira (which are *really frightening*), Peter makes it clear that they were not obligated to sell their property and give the money to the community.[13] Second, living a life in a very close community structure is not impossible today, if people decide they want to do so. While we are not recommending a communal life, examples of this lifestyle exist today. If you want to learn about some of the disciplines and blessings that come from living in close community, we would recommend reading *Life Together* by Dietrich Bonhoeffer.

We are not advocating a communal Christian Community, but we do firmly believe that in order to become all that God wants us to be, we need to draw closer together as a body of believers. We need to move more to a model where we are more closely involved with the lives of the Christians in our community than we are today. This takes vulnerability, which is another thing our modern culture often is not comfortable with.

A Commitment to Christian Community will in all likelihood mean committing to (and joining) a local church and making the decision to become involved and stay involved in that church. That will likely mean attending scheduled services, participating in ministries of the church (both to others in the church and by outreach to people not attending the church), and joining small groups. But if those things are just additional activities, we will miss the point. More importantly, a Commitment to Christian Community will cause us to open up to, trust, and rely upon others to a point where the relationships become meaningful and the activities become the natural result of those relationships.

A real Commitment to Christian Community will also involve a commitment to stay involved even when things don't go your way. Brad has been the senior pastor of Lakeshore Church for more than twenty-five years and I have attended that same church for more than twenty-four years. During that time we have both had many things that didn't go the way we wanted, and we have each had multiple opportunities to leave the church and go somewhere else. However, because we chose to stay involved with our church, we have grown stronger in our faith and are able to develop and enjoy long-term relationships with people we know better and have been able to affect more deeply than would have been the case had we moved to another church congregation every 6.6 years.[14]

For all of these reasons and more, it is an important spiritual milestone when we decide to commit to a community of believers, and the point that each of us makes that decision will be a Defining Moment in our lives.

When I think of what a community of believers should look like, I think of a group of six couples from our church, but in reality, as you might expect, that group is led and held together by the six wives, who call themselves the Six Chicks. These couples met nearly twenty years ago during a series of mission trips to Nicaragua, and they developed strong friendships through serving there together. However, the Six Chicks have gone beyond friendship. Even though they no longer all attend the same church, they have forged a bond among themselves that is unbreakable and the envy of many of their other friends.

These six remarkable ladies all have different talents, which are manifestations of the gifts of the Spirit described in 1 Corinthians 12. Yet they have functioned together as ministry partners for nearly two decades without missing a beat. For years they have had a regular Friday morning prayer call which keeps them in touch with their own personal needs and the needs of their families and friends. They have led mission and tourism trips, led and participated in Bible studies, taught classes, and have served in multiple ministry capacities at their churches, both in leadership and nonleadership roles. By virtue of their relationship, they have witnessed numerous healings and other miracles; have seen people make commitments to Christ; have helped friends and family work through marital problems, deaths, and other personal difficulties; and have stood as prayer warriors for the benefit of many.

However, don't think that they are just six old ladies with their hair in buns and wearing tennis shoes. During the period of their relationship, most of the Six Chicks have (or have had) successful careers, have raised children, and have had to manage the normal day-to-day responsibilities that we all face. But despite their life responsibilities, they also find time to serve in ministry together, take girls' trips together (and once in a great while invite their husbands), have more birthday lunches and dinners each year than a group of six should reasonably have, and enjoy shopping trips, girls' nights out, and even an occasional sleepover.

But most significantly, these ladies have impacted each other immensely. They have grown closer to the Lord and have expanded their areas of ministry and influence. If you asked each of them, they would say that their decision to commit to each other as a group of believers has been a Defining Moment in their lives. The kind of relationship they enjoy and experience is what we can all develop if we truly make a Commitment to Christian Community.

CHAPTER 6

Moments That Change Our Worlds

"The 2 most important days in your life are the day you are born,
and the day you discover why you were born."

—LOU HOLTZ

In this chapter we will be talking about jobs and careers, but most importantly about finding our purpose in life. The Bible teaches that all work is important and worth doing well. Ecclesiastes 9:10 (NKJV) tells us that, "Whatever your hand finds to do, do it with all your might...," and Colossians 3:23 (NIV) sounds a similar theme by saying, "Whatever you do, work at it with all your heart, as working for the Lord, not for human masters."

One of the beautiful things about life is that we all are different. We have different interests, different talents, and different qualities that allow us to succeed in life. We see in the Bible and in our life experience that all talents and abilities are necessary to make our world work. We need builders, doctors and nurses, chefs, waiters and waitresses, pilots, drivers, teachers, librarians, superintendents and lunchroom workers, bankers, engineers, painters, landscapers and gardeners, handymen (and women), construction workers, farmers, ranchers, forest rangers, parents, preachers, lawyers, secretaries, mayors, clerks, and people working in innumerable other capacities for our world to function well.

We believe that God has a distinct purpose for each of us in life.[1] If that is true, then it's safe to say that we will feel a lack of purpose until we discover what His purpose is for us. And just as we noted above that it takes an innumerable variety of workers to make our world function well, God has gifted different people with a special sense of purpose in each of those areas. When we discover that purpose, our lives are changed. From that point forward it is just a matter of pursuing that purpose and refining the mission you have been called to. That road can lead you on a lot of twists and turns and can take you into careers and into worlds that you didn't know even existed—and with your future at stake, you don't want to miss or mess up these Defining Moments. A primary purpose of this chapter is to help you find and fulfill your purpose for the remainder of your life.

Growing up, I never even considered being a lawyer. My ideas about my future were limited by the world I was raised in, and since the world around me was very limited, I had a limited view of where I could go and what I could do. The world I knew was rural, and it seemed to me that my career options were limited to farming, operating a small business, or teaching high school. While farm life may seem idyllic to many, the multiple summers I spent on tractors and combines reducing hundred-acre fields by ever-shrinking concentric loops convinced me that the farm life was not to be part of my future.

I went to college with no real sense of direction but with a general idea that I wanted to be a high school history teacher. As semesters went by, I was enjoying my college years (and too often enjoying them too much) but had no real sense of direction and no thought of a career. Then one day during my junior year in college, I went to talk with my Russian history professor, Dr. Repko. He commented that he thought I would make a good lawyer, and after several lengthy conversations with him, my world began to change. Prior to that I had always thought in terms of getting a job after college, but after my conversations with Dr. Repko, I saw that a career with multiple possible life paths was a possibility.

The suggestion and career counseling I received from my history professor was one of the most significant Defining Moments in my life. Although at that time in my life I did not have the sense of process (RARE) that I have outlined in this book, without even realizing it then, I followed the steps of dealing with that moment perfectly. First, I *recognized* that I was facing a decision that could change my life forever by shifting me from a possible teaching career to a legal career. Next, I *analyzed* the benefits of making that decision and realized that it would be a good choice for me. Finally, I *responded effectively* by shifting the remainder of my college career to preparation for law school and enrolled in the JD/MBA program at the University of Notre Dame.

That Defining Moment and my response to it was a moment that changed my world. Rather than returning to a rural community after college, I was catapulted into a world and life that I didn't even know existed. None of my family members had been lawyers or worked in the legal profession, so I had no idea what I would encounter. However, I soon learned that, as Dr. Repko predicted, I was perfectly suited to be an attorney, and that it was the path that God had destined for me.

In this chapter, we will examine Defining Moments in our careers and how each of us can take steps to maximize those opportunities. However, at the outset of this discussion it is important to note that we are not assessing any greater value to one career compared to another. As noted above (and as noted in the song by Robert Palmer), "it takes every kinda people to make the world go 'round." A successful career doesn't need to fit within any mold. In fact, because God destines each of us for specific purposes, every career will be different. In writing this book, we are speaking from our own career experiences, but fully recognize the importance of all careers. Further, the Bible teaches that all work should be done to the best of our ability and to the glory of God.[2]

Decisions we face in our professional lives need to be treated like any other Defining Moments. We need to recognize the moment, analyze and evaluate it carefully, and then respond effectively. This chapter will look at some key principles involved in setting our professional destinies.

A JOB IS GREAT—A CAREER IS BETTER

Work is ordained by God and is one of our primary purposes on earth. In fact, when God created the earth and all that is in it, the Bible tells us that God put man in the Garden of Eden to work it and take care of it.[3] We were designed to find great fulfillment, joy, and purpose in working.

People often talk about looking for a job, and a job is a good and valuable thing. We should be thankful for the opportunity to work and support ourselves and our families. However, a job becomes most fulfilling when it is woven into a career. Analyzing a job opportunity in and of itself without also considering the long-term, sometimes lifelong perspective that accompanies it is a mistake. When considering a job, we should be evaluating it in the context of a career.

A career can be described as an occupation undertaken for a significant period of a person's life and with opportunities for progress.[4] That definition is helpful but doesn't convey the full meaning of the term. When we think about a career, we are thinking about something that brings purpose to our lives, that fulfills our inner need to feel that our lives have had meaning, and that we have had an impact on the world around us. Our careers should allow us to incorporate our life values into our work and to be a means for expressing our interests and unique personalities. In the best case, we would feel that our career was consistent with God's purpose for us. If so, then later in our lives we should have a sense of accomplishment and the satisfaction that comes from knowledge that our lives have impacted the world around us.

Does God have a purpose for each of us? Absolutely. In Jeremiah 29:11 (NIV) it says, "'For I know the plans I have for you,' declares the Lord, 'plans to prosper you and not to harm you, plans to give you hope and a future.'" That purpose and that future should be incorporated into our careers. Other verses support this concept of a unique purpose for each of us.[5] One of the things people often struggle with is identifying that purpose, and the point at which you identify God's purpose for you will be a Defining Moment in your life!

From time to time we all wish God would audibly tell us His purpose for our lives or what He wants us to do for a career. Unfortunately, that doesn't happen often, but there are things we can consider to better understand His calling. One of the most important is to consider who we are and what interests us. The Bible says that God gives us the desires of our hearts.[6] Therefore, if you are naturally inclined to enjoy certain types of work, that may be consistent with God's purpose for you. Similarly, consider the training and education you have received and the opportunities that have come across your path. If you are sincerely seeking God's direction, He will lead you to the place He has called you.

After you have chosen a career, it is important to do everything within your power and control to pursue it and maximize the opportunities. You need to seek the education and training needed to succeed in that career. Remember, God calls YOU to do something for His Kingdom; He doesn't do it for you. As you move through your career it won't always be easy but it will be rewarding.

I have four children but only one daughter. There have been few things more exciting or worrisome than realizing that my daughter had met the young man she was planning to marry. Sarah had a courtship that is extremely uncommon in this day and age. She met Jordan one night during a summer visit to North Dakota and almost exactly two years later was married after developing a relationship through letters and phone calls despite a physical separation of more than one thousand miles. It was truly the stuff that romance novels are made of!

In one of the few conversations I had with Jordan before he and Sarah were engaged I asked him his goals and dreams for the future. He told me that he was planning to attend a seminary in Vancouver, British Columbia, thereby further separating me from my little girl. And if that wasn't enough, after giving it some thought he told me that if he could script his future he would return to North Dakota to farm with his family and be a part-time pastor in a small rural church.

Those goals sent chills down my spine for multiple reasons, and I left that conversation hoping that he would come to his senses. I had fled the farm life, knowing that it was not at all what I wanted to do, and here he was choosing it for himself and my daughter, a girl that had spent her entire life in Texas and had no clue what North Dakota winters could be like.

As Jordan was nearing the end of his seminary education, we had the opportunity to speak about his future plans, and I suggested that it might be good for him to work in a larger church to get experience as he began his career. I was surprised when he told me that he really had no desire to pastor a large urban church and didn't really see that in his future. For me, this was the opposite view I had pursued in my life. My professional life had been about taking jobs to get good experience and then building a larger law practice and continuously setting larger goals. When Jordan left school, I wondered how he could provide for my daughter, as I knew that neither farming (especially in North Dakota) nor preaching (especially in a small rural church) would be lucrative.

Despite *my* anxiety, I sensed that Jordan was completely at peace with *his* career choice, and his primary concerns seemed to be with how God would cause it to happen, not whether it was a good choice. I wish I could say that I immediately felt confidence in his goals, but I didn't. I knew my daughter better than he did at that time (or so I thought), and I didn't see any way that she would be either a farmer's wife or a pastor's wife, and he was asking her to do both.

Our initial conversation was more than fifteen years ago. Today my son-in-law is doing exactly what he told me he wanted to do—farming with his family and serving as the pastor at a rural Lutheran Church. I have learned so much while watching this come about. However, as amazing as anything, I have seen the impact of making a career choice and sticking to it. I thought it was important for my son-in-law to get a good job, but Jordan knew he wanted a career. Through this, I have seen God give a young man the desires of his heart, and have seen him experience the true joy of seeing a career develop and mature—a joy I experienced in a very different way.

It hasn't always or often been easy for them, but seeing Jordan move into a career that allows him to fulfill God's purpose for his life is so much more rewarding than simply taking a job and earning a salary would have been. And my daughter? Well, she's amazing! Never a rigid planner, she has enjoyed discovering the story of her life as God is telling it. She injects herself into her small community in many ways, which she finds very fulfilling. God has led her on a journey that I can only thank Him for, as I have seen her mature into a true Proverbs 31 woman of God. As a friend of mine once told me, sometimes when we have trouble trusting God, it's almost like He likes to show off and says, "Watch this!" just to let us know He has things under control. Watching their lives develop has been one of those times for me.

TRAIN TO BE READY

We all want to find that sweet spot in our life where we know that we are doing exactly what God has called us to do. We want to be fulfilled in life. We want to know we are making a difference in the world. However, all that desiring, hoping, and dreaming often has the unintended consequence of making us wait too long for it all to happen, and that can frustrate our desires, hopes, and dreams from actually coming to fruition. I have often seen people so earnestly waiting for God to direct and lead them somewhere exactly in the manner they expected that they were unable to ever start down that career path.

Our futures are intertwined with and dependent upon our pasts. We cannot proceed directly to the end result without a lot of work and preparation. We all know that, but we don't always apply it. I'm not an athlete, but the sports analogy is recognized by everyone and seems to work so well here. An athlete does not become elite without hours, weeks, months, and years spent training, building, and advancing their skills. All the weekends spent taking a child to YMCA soccer or Pee Wee baseball seem to reap minimal rewards until that child is able to succeed at the next level. Then all the hours spent running drills, taking batting practice, or building endurance seem to mean little until the scholarship offers start to come in. And on and on it goes as the young man or woman climbs the ladder of athletic success until one day that person is at the top of his or her game and they look back and realize that all their daily decisions to commit their work and effort paid off.

That same principle applies to all of us as we travel the road to reaching our career goals, beginning with our education and training. I had little interest in high school, but as I moved closer and closer to entering my career, school became more interesting and I became more committed to studying to succeed. Yet if I would not have studied hard enough in high school to get into college or if I would not have worked and studied hard enough in college to get into law school, I never would have reached my career goal of being an attorney. Even though I was not where I wanted to go, I kept working toward it.

That same principle applies as we start working in our adult lives. Few people start their professional careers with glamorous jobs. Usually it is just the opposite. We start in low-level positions which seem drudgingly boring with little glamour. However, as we perform those tasks faithfully, we not only build character, but we also move into different opportunities, the work becomes more interesting, and recognition is more regularly achieved. We do all this hoping that one day we will look back over the career path we've taken and realize that all that work was worth it, that we achieved a meaningful and satisfying career, and we can see how God led us through the difficult times to get to the place He intended for us to be.

All of that education, training, and hard work are part of what we do as we are walking in the pathway of God's perfect will. It is important not to grow impatient or disillusioned and move out of where we *need* to be, and we end up missing God's perfect will for our lives and accepting second best.

All of that training prepares us to be ready and willing to move to the next step when the opportunity is available. Earlier in this book we addressed how fear can prevent us from making good decisions at Defining Moments in our lives. This is equally true when we reach critical junctures in our professional lives. These are times when we are balancing our current place in life against what the future may hold, and so often there is a fear of taking the step that can change our professional lives forever because of that fear of the unknown.

The Bible tells us that we need to be ready to move when the opportunity arises. In Luke 9 there are two examples of people saying that they wanted to follow Christ but wanted to delay. One man asked to first go bury his father and the other wanted to go back and say goodbye to his family. In both instances the Lord's response was to tell them that they should come follow Him rather than delay.[7]

A great example of being ready to take the next step is in 1 Kings 19, when the prophet Elijah calls Elisha to follow him. The Bible doesn't tell us about Elisha's life prior to this encounter, but from the context of the passage we can assume that he was a farmer working at home with his parents. I think it is also safe to assume that he knew he had a different destiny in his future because of the nature and alacrity of his response. Elijah came to Elisha and cast his mantle upon him, thereby indicating that Elisha was to follow him. Elisha acted quickly and decisively, and his actions make it clear that he *recognized* this as a Defining Moment in his life. He killed the oxen that he had been plowing with, cooked them over a fire built with the harnesses and other equipment used to drive the oxen, and left to become Elijah's servant. His actions evidenced his complete commitment to his calling and left him no possibility of turning back. The remainder of the story of Elisha's life shows us that this was a great example of a Defining Moment that changed his world forever. Rather than being one of many farmers he became God's prophet for his generation! We need to trust our preparation and have that same willingness to act when the next step is presented to us.

EXPECT TO BE BLESSED

Like Elisha, we may need to make a decision to move forward in a way that will forever change our world without regard to whether or not there is a safety net to fall back on. That can be scary. However, the anxiety of making those decisions will be tempered if we go forward with the confidence that if we are moving into a place that God intends us to be, He will provide for us. Again, this is a biblical promise. In Psalm 37:25, the writer says that he has never seen the righteous forsaken or his seed begging bread. The Bible makes it clear that one of the things we are to do during our time on earth is to work. If you are walking in His will for your professional life, the promises of God's provision are there for you too!

However, sometimes Christians seem to get the idea that it is somehow wrong to ask God to bless our work and reward us for our work. That idea is not biblical, and in fact, is contradictory to Scripture.

First Chronicles 4:10 recites a prayer by the Old Testament character, Jabez. In this prayer, Jabez asks God to "bless me and enlarge my territory." In the small, wonderful book by Dr. Bruce H. Wilkinson, *The Prayer of Jabez,* Wilkinson describes the blessing that is being requested as an impartation of supernatural favor. "When we ask for God's blessing, we're not asking for more of what we could get for ourselves. We're crying out for the wonderful unlimited goodness that only God has the power to know about or give to us."[8] After that prayer, the Bible goes on to say that God granted his request.

That passage and many other biblical passages should give us great confidence. When you arrive at a Defining Moment in your professional life, recognize and analyze it. After analysis if you decide it is an opportunity that should be pursued, ask God to bless your endeavor with success, and have the confidence to know that if you commit your work to God and pursue it with diligence, God will grant your request!

———

During my years at Oral Roberts University, President Oral Roberts frequently spoke on the biblical principle he called Seed Faith. The idea was that if you planted seeds into the Kingdom of God, whether time, treasure, or talent, God would reward your efforts. There are many scriptural passages supporting this doctrine. There are also many instances of ministers abusing these Scriptures and using them for advancement of their own ministries. I bring this up not to argue the point or try to resolve the theological issues involved, but just to say that the teaching impacted me.

My law partner and I started our own law practice with a bang in August of 1989 (more about that in chapter 10). By January of 1990, we only had a single active project in our office and only limited prospects for new business. The future of our law firm, which started with such great promise, now appeared so bleak.

In January of 1990, our pastor invited my wife and me to a special luncheon one Sunday after church. At that meeting, he presented his vision for the future ministry of our church and asked each person at the luncheon to make a special gift for the ministry and to expect God to bless us in return. As I sat and listened, I felt the Holy Spirit guiding me to make a special gift. The problem was that our law firm had hit a dry spell and Mary and I were at the end of our financial rope. In fact, we only had about $1,000 available, a hefty mortgage payment, and three young children to support. Our personal financial pressures and my responsibilities were heavy on my mind, but God was working on my heart.

At that moment, I remembered all of the Seed Faith teachings I had learned. My analysis was simple: One option was to give nothing, spend my $1,000 over the next couple weeks, and then I would be broke. The other option was to give the $1,000 that day, be broke immediately, and trust God to bless my gift. Looking back today, more than thirty years later, I am amazed at how simple the decision seemed. I gave the money and like Jabez, asked God to "enlarge my territory," or, in my world's vernacular, to expand our law firm's business. Upon giving that gift, I had no safety net.

The results were astounding. Two days after that Sunday lunch meeting, I received a call from a new client. Their attorney had recently retired and they wondered if I could represent them. Two weeks after that, I received a call from another new client asking us to represent them on a major real estate acquisition. Thirty years later, our law firm still represents both of those clients, and we have never been without business since!

CHAPTER 7

Moments That Matter to Us

"...that is our calling: to show that there is
a reality in personal relationship,
and not just words about it."

—Francis Schaeffer

A very close friend of mine once told me that the Bible doesn't require us to be happy but only says that we will experience joy by following Christ. (As you might imagine, his personality was more of an Eeyore than a Tigger.) Nonetheless, most of us seek happiness, and it is generally conducive to each of us living better lives individually and creating a better society communally. But happiness doesn't just happen. Some people say that happiness is *a choice*; however, I think that more accurately it is the result of *multiple choices* throughout the course of our lives. In this chapter, we will look at several common decisions we all face in our personal lives that will greatly enhance our happiness and contentment if we recognize, analyze, and respond effectively to them—thereby making them Defining Moments in our lives.

CHOOSE RELATIONSHIPS OVER SOLITUDE

Friends and good friendships have a huge impact upon our lives and our general happiness and contentment in life. For those reasons it is important that we seek and develop good friendships. A recent publication by the Mayo Clinic Staff stated, "Good friends are good for your health." The publication went on to list five significant benefits of friendship, stating that friends can (i) increase your sense of belonging and purposes, (ii) boost your happiness and reduce your stress, (iii) improve your self-confidence and self-worth, (iv) help you cope with traumatic situations, and (v) encourage you to change or avoid unhealthy lifestyle habits.[1]

Conversely, not having good friends and strong friendships can have a negative impact upon our lives and our happiness and contentment. The Health Resources and Services Administration (HRSA) within the U.S. Department of Health and Human Services is the primary federal agency responsible for improving access to health care and enhancing health systems for people who are geographically isolated and/or economically or medically vulnerable.[2] The HRSA has stated that loneliness and social isolation can be as damaging to health as smoking fifteen cigarettes a day. It says that living alone, being unmarried, no participation in social groups, fewer friends, and strained relationships are not only all *risk factors for premature mortality,* but also increase risk for loneliness.[3]

We cannot overemphasize the importance of good friends and, as noted above, the evidence supports it. St. Thomas Aquinas recognized this, stating, "There is nothing on this earth more to be prized than true friendship." Yet so many people feel lonely and friendless, living their lives in isolation. However, it doesn't have to be that way. Each of us can reach out and build relationships that will improve our contentment as well as our overall health. Sometimes we face decisions, large and small, that will establish or restore friendships and that prove to be Defining

Moments in our lives because those friends and relationships can have a permanent impact upon our lives and our destinies.

If friendships are so important, let's take a look at some principles that we should consider in developing and maintaining friendships:

1. *Choose your friends wisely.* There are many verses in the Bible that advise of the importance of choosing good friends, but Proverbs 13:20 condenses it quite clearly: "He that walketh with wise men shall be wise: but a companion of fools shall be destroyed." We tend to become like the people we associate with. Consequently, the choice of a single person to be a close friend can be a Defining Moment in our lives. Spending time with friends with good character traits will cause us to improve our character. Conversely, hanging with friends of bad character can lead to bad consequences. For those of us that are fans of *Lonesome Dove,* this principle is laid out in Captain Augustus McCrae's last words to Jake Spoon before Jake was hung: "Ride with an outlaw, die with him."[4] While in most instances the consequences of bad friendships are not quite so harsh, those bad friendships are to be avoided, and good ones sought after, in all instances.

2. *Value existing friendships.* A long-standing business principle is that existing customers are more valuable than new customers. In fact, it has been estimated that it costs five times more to attract a new customer than it does to retain an existing one.[5] This principle translates well to friendships also. Existing friends are valuable, and new friends are hard to find. Yet so often it seems that people don't value the existing friendships they have, and the failure to value those relationships ignores the history we have with those long-term friends. Treat your existing friends like you would want them to treat you, without worrying about reciprocity, and in most cases those friendships will grow stronger. At times when you are lonely or looking for a friend,

think of people you haven't contacted in a while and seek to rebuild the relationships.

> Old, dormant friendships
> are like veins of gold,
> if mined they give access
> to the treasure they hold.

3. *Friendship as a ministry tool.* If loneliness is indeed an epidemic, as stated by the HRSA, each of us should look at friendship and reaching out to others as an incredible ministry opportunity. If you know people that are lonely and don't have a lot of friends, reach out to them and build those friendships. Not only can you relieve their loneliness, but you can also mentor them to make good decisions and improve their lives. Along the way you will probably learn something from them also.

***

A good friendship was one of the most impactful Defining Moments in Brad's life. Here is his description of the relationship:

I met James Bowen in May of 1984 soon after my arrival to Shreveport, Louisiana, where I had just been hired as the student pastor at Life Tabernacle Church. At the time I had no church ministry experience. James introduced himself to me and then graciously volunteered to lead worship for the youth services. With a 6'5" frame and legendary reputation as one of the best former high school quarterbacks in the city, I concluded that it would be wise to take him up on his offer, which was a decision that positively impacted my life.

James knew that I had no idea what I was doing as a youth minister, but he came alongside me and helped me learn to become a better pastor to the students. He stood up for me on many occasions and supported me even when I made poor decisions. James volunteered for the most difficult tasks, he helped plan our biggest events, and he was there for me in the most challenging of times. That level of loyalty, integrity, and faithfulness helped create a lifelong bond of friendship between us.

I was asked by our senior pastor to direct a youth camp and turned to James for assistance. We worked closely together, and our friendship was used by God to create a powerful ministry tool. James helped me plan that year's youth camp, and he personally developed a novel system for building unity and creating multiple fun activities for the campers. James became known as the Games Guy and year after year he helped make our youth camp better.

The popularity of our youth camp was one reason that I was asked to join the staff at Christ For The Nations in Dallas (CFNI) to serve as their youth ministry director in 1990. One of my primary tasks was to help organize the initial *Youth for the Nations* (YFN) convention. This was going to be a signature event for CFNI, and I felt all the burden of responsibility that went with having to meet those expectations. I needed help, and I turned to James. Always a true friend, he helped come up with what we now call The Nations Games—an integral part of the YFN experience, and that first event was a great success. Had it not been for my friend's intervention in my time of need, *Youth for the Nations* would be totally different today, and, in fact, it may not even exist.

To date, over 100,000 students have attended *Youth for the Nations,* and many of those young people are now in key leadership and ministry positions around the world. *Youth for the Nations* will celebrate its thirtieth anniversary as of the writing of this book. Had I not met James and had he not befriended me, it would likely have been a much different story.

More than two decades after that first YFN event, we were privileged to hire James' son, Sean, as our media director at Lakeshore Church. The quality video content Sean produces reflects the same values of his father. The loyalty, work ethic, and excellence he brings to the team has helped us reach more people through online media than we ever dreamed.

My friendship with James Bowen changed the trajectory of my ministry (and may have saved my career in ministry), and his influence continues to affect my life for the better. God knew exactly the type of friend that I needed to become the minister He called me to be, and I am thankful to Him for providing James.

James Bowen and I remain good friends today, almost forty years after our initial meeting.

MARRIAGE AND FAMILY

There is no more significant decision you can make in your personal life (excluding religious Defining Moments for purposes of this discussion) than getting married and having children. We include both of these together because they are so intertwined, and because children are usually one of the results of a marriage. However, we certainly understand that many people have very happy and successful marriages without having children, or have children but are unmarried. In any event, however, the choice of a life partner and bringing children into our lives are Defining Moments in anyone's life.

At the beginning of the book of beginnings, God sets forth His intentions and His plan for marriage. By looking at a few critical verses, the significance of the decisions we make regarding marriage becomes apparent. By stating that, "It is not good that the man should be alone,"[6] God is saying that we are missing something important in our lives if we live alone. Further, in that same verse God goes on to state that He will make him a help meet for man and thereafter creates the woman, Eve, to be with Adam. By God's creation of a woman we can understand that it is His perfect will for a marriage to be between a man and a woman.

The statement that God has created Eve as a help meet has been interpreted in many ways throughout history and unfortunately is often interpreted based primarily upon the viewpoint of the person speaking on the subject. When we look at these words in Hebrew (*'ezer kanegdo*) and the context in which they were written, the best interpretation is to treat the words which are translated into "help meet" in the King James Version of the Bible, as a "strong, mighty counterbalance."

To understand this terminology in the context of the marriage relationship it is also helpful to realize that when Eve was created, not only was she created for Adam, but Adam had already been created for her. The woman was not created to be either the man's servant or his overlord, but rather someone to walk together with him as they journey through life and to provide him help and support. However, it is important to note that the concept of a "strong, mighty counterbalance" necessarily incorporates the concept of mutuality. The man is to provide similar help and support to his wife. Brad and I are both blessed to have wives that provide that counterbalance, and we strive to give that same reciprocal blessing to them as well.

A few verses later, the Bible says, "Therefore shall a man leave his father and mother, and shall cleave unto his wife: and they shall be one flesh."[7] This verse, which is repeated by Christ[8] and by the apostle Paul,[9] emphasizes two major points. First, it identifies the covenant relationship between a man and a woman that arises in a marriage relationship. By becoming "one flesh," there is to be unity between them from that point forward.

The second major point from this verse is that a man is to leave his mother and father and cleave to his wife. This separation from our past and beginning a new life together is of major significance. By entering into marriage, we are saying that the new relationship we are beginning is now more important than any family relationships we lived with prior to that point, and that will impact our future forever.

The Bible makes it clear, and reality proves, that the decision to marry someone presents each of us with a Defining Moment in our life. The impact of this particular Defining Moment makes it especially important that this moment is to be recognized, analyzed carefully, and decided correctly. The RARE principles specified earlier in chapter 4 will provide a basis for dealing with this critical Defining Moment. When a person considers marriage, he or she should focus significant effort on *analyzing* the Defining Moment they are facing. Some of the things to be considered include the following:

1. Is your future spouse a person that is a friend? If you will be living with that person for the rest of your life, you had better get along!

2. Do you get along with your future spouse's family? Even though you leave your father and mother when you get married, you will be dealing with them for years to come.

3. Do you have similar dreams, goals, and objectives?

4. Do you have similar religious beliefs and convictions?

5. Do you both agree on whether or not to have children and at least some general agreement about how many?

The list of considerations could go on and on.

While there are many things that should be considered in the decision process regarding marriage, we would caution anyone to not put undue emphasis on emotions or money. There is probably no Defining Moment you will face which is more fraught with emotional influence than deciding who or whether to marry. While emotions will undoubtedly have some influence, following your heart alone, is bad, nonbiblical advice that can lead you into many difficult situations. Additionally, we hear so often that people don't have enough money to get married. In many situations, that is often a concern more related to your spending habits, career choice, and work ethic than to the decision to get married.

If you are married, the decision whether or not to have children will likely have already been made, or at least general principles will have been agreed upon. It is important to note that children are part of God's plan,[10] children are a heritage and reward from God,[11] and that children have a special place in God's heart and plan.[12] With all that and more in God's Word about the blessings of children, we sometimes wonder why couples don't have more of them.

When it comes to your personal life, the person you marry can have the greatest impact on your future. Yet the decision is often fraught with uncertainty. That doesn't have to be the case as God is very capable of leading us to the right person. Here is Brad's story of how he connected with his wife:

———————

I met Denise during our first semester of Bible school. Her sister, Elaine, introduced us, and it was not love at first sight. After a couple social gatherings, Denise told her roommates that she could never date a guy like Brad Howard. I believe she used words like dull and boring to describe her initial perception of me. I admit, it was a legitimate assessment. If not for staying connected through mutual friends, she may have avoided me altogether.

I took advantage of every opportunity to sit next to Denise in class. I wouldn't admit that I liked her, but I did. I kept trying to convince myself that I didn't move to Dallas to meet girls. Like Jake and Elwood in *The Blues Brothers,* I felt I was on a mission from God, and I was not going to let anything or anyone get in my way. In retrospect, I was being played. Like a hooked fish, I was being reeled in just a little at a time. God's plan for my life included a lot more than a ministerial degree.

Our family backgrounds were radically different. Denise grew up in an extremely healthy home with Christ-centered values. Her parents were the Ward and June Cleaver of their community. Her father was a successful banker, and her mother was a confident pillar of faith who made sure her five beautiful daughters had everything they needed. My family, on the other hand, was a mess. I had no concept of healthy lifestyles, especially regarding marriage and family. We lacked structure and struggled hard to make ends meet following the divorce of my parents. From the time I was sixteen and continuing through Bible school, I worked a full-time job just to help pay the bills. These two opposite worlds were destined to collide.

Our families lived close, less than thirty minutes from my house to hers. I asked Denise if I could give her a ride home for Christmas break, and she asked me over for dinner. Dale, her father, was cordial but stern. Her sisters were friendly and had lots of questions. But I believe it was the moment I met her mother that sealed my fate. I didn't know it at the time but Denise's mom, Elna, had always told her that she would grow up and marry a pastor. Elna had been praying for me for a very long time. The meal was great, the visit was wonderful, but the strangest thing happened the very next night.

I dreamed I married Denise. Now let me clarify one thing—I'm not a big fan of dream interpretation but this one was different. It was all so vivid and detailed. The little white church with a steeple, the steps leading up to the entrance, the stained glass windows…a Norman Rockwell-esque scene, but I was petrified. So much so that I woke drenched in sweat but extremely relieved to know it was all just a dream. I didn't tell Denise about the dream at the time, but I did let her know on the way home that I was not at all interested in anything beyond a friendship. In retrospect, I am glad that God had other plans.

The next summer we ended up on the same school-sponsored mission trip (totally unplanned) to Jamaica. Our faculty leader divided us into three different teams, each with a specific ministry assignment for our month-long mission. Up until a few days before we left, Denise and I were not on the same team. But in a dramatic turn of events, everything changed, as Denise and I became our own team. It was during our ministry time together in Jamaica that I realized how much I loved Denise and wanted to spend the rest of my life with her.

When we arrived back at the school the next semester, we signed up for preengagement counseling. Our counselor helped confirm our desire to pursue a long-term relationship. Before I asked Denise to marry me, I asked for her father's blessing. As well, I was able to write to my father and get his blessing. The letter of blessing he wrote me is a treasure that I keep in my office to this day.

Denise and I were married on June 2, 1984, in Clayton, Texas, at that little white church I saw in my dream, and my life was changed forever. More than that, however, Denise has helped shape me into being a different person, with confidence and strengths I never had before meeting her. In that way and others, Denise has changed my character.

Left to my own devices, I would have missed the most important Defining Moment of my personal life. My marriage to Denise is absolutely the best thing that's ever happened to me. God knew that to fulfill my destiny and become the person He wanted me to be, I needed Denise beside me. We've worked together on every major ministry event and mission endeavor during our years together. She is the reason for the strength of our marriage, the stability of our family, and the duration of our ministry.

I truly know the meaning of the verse, "He who finds a wife finds a good thing, And obtains favor from the LORD."[13]

STAYING MARRIED

We just finished a discussion of Marriage and Family, so it might seem a bit redundant to now focus our discussion on Staying Married. However, it seems that getting married doesn't have a strong correlation to staying married anymore. Recent statistics showed that while divorces in the United States declined in the period from 2008-2018, there were still nearly half as many divorces as there were new marriages in America in 2018.[14]

The high divorce rate in our nation continues despite the fact that the consequences of divorce generally have a significant negative impact on persons getting divorced as well as on their families. In one study, results showed that divorced respondents' wealth starts falling four years before divorce and they experience an average wealth drop of 77 percent.[15] The impact of divorce on children can also be very negative and can result in children who go through the divorce suffering many negative experiences, including mental health problems, behavior problems, and poor academic performance.[16]

Aside from the many negative consequences of divorce on the married couple and their children that are reflected in multiple studies, as Christians we also need to face the fact that divorce is contrary to biblical teachings. To be more direct, in many (*but not all*) instances, divorce is sin. Yet despite this teaching, in our nation today the statistics regarding divorce by Christians are only slightly better than those among nonbelievers.

Our purpose in discussing divorce in this book is not to present a thorough sociological study or to even do an in-depth theological analysis of the topic. Rather, it is to point out that due to the many negative consequences of divorce, the decision to stay married, to choose not to divorce, can be a Defining Moment in the lives of those confronted with this decision.

The decision to stay married and work through difficult times is also a Defining Moment because it is reflective of our character. As noted above, the covenant relationship arising through marriage is identified multiple places in the Bible, and the covenant nature of this relationship remains today. When making the traditional Christian wedding vows, a man and woman reaffirm that covenant by saying things like, "I take thee to be my wedded husband/wife for better, for worse, for richer, for poorer, in sickness and in health, till death do us part." Breaking those vows often reflects character issues—and likewise, so does honoring them.

The decision to stay married, if handled properly and coupled with counseling and behavioral changes that will repair and restore the marriage relationship to what God intended, can literally be a life-changing decision. That choice can avoid many of the negative consequences of divorce, such as guilt, negative impact upon children, and the financial hardship that often accompanies or results from divorce. Additionally, if the couple works to restore their marriage, they can experience the joyful relationship that God intends marriage to be, and the satisfaction of a rewarding life journey and maturing together with their dearest friend. As significant as the decision to marry can be, the decision to stay married and make the marriage work as God intended can be just as significant.

Years ago, I lived near a couple that were dear friends of ours (we will call them Jack and Jill for this discussion). Jack was successful in his business, Jill was beautiful, both physically and in her personality, and they had children that seemingly succeeded at everything they did. A perfect American family. Yet unbeknownst to many, Jack and Jill were going through an extremely rocky period in their marriage. For a couple in their early forties, some of the problems they were experiencing were not unique to them but were common to many people we have known. However, also like many couples, especially Christian couples, they were able to keep up a façade that prevented most of their acquaintances from realizing that they were facing a significant marital crisis.

Their problems became more evident when they went through a public disagreement that made it apparent to many of their friends that they had serious problems. They sought Christian counseling, but nothing seemed to allow them to bridge the chasm that had developed in their relationship. In fact, it seemed so hopeless that even their pastor told them that sometimes marriages just didn't work out and that they may want to consider a divorce. Some of their family members gave them the same advice. They were both young and successful, and starting over almost seemed easy.

Their problems finally got to a point where I felt I no longer had the luxury of avoiding involvement. It was very difficult, but I went to meet with them and we had a very direct conversation. I told them what they already knew, that it was not God's will that they get a divorce, and that they both needed to make fundamental behavioral changes for their marriage to work.

Jack and Jill faced that Defining Moment in their lives where they could have chosen one of two ways to proceed. Divorce and a restart seemed easy, and certainly they would not have been the first Christian family or even the first Christian family in their church to choose that route. The other alternative, staying married, required work, and lots of it, but they knew that was God's will. It wasn't easy, but thankfully Jack and Jill made the choice to put in the necessary effort to stay married and to make their marriage a success.

It was one of the most rewarding moments of my life, when years later Jack came to me and thanked me for meeting with them that night. They remain married today, and can give a testimony of God's restoration to all that will listen.

IT'S YOUR LIFE, TAKE CONTROL OF IT!

The topics we have covered in this chapter are important, but in fact they are only a few of the many things that influence our lives and our happiness, contentment, and feelings of fulfillment. We could talk about many other life decisions and Defining Moments each of us may face that will have a huge impact on our personal lives. Things like where we choose to live, exercise and maintaining physical fitness, involvement in our children's lives, relationships with grandchildren, recreational activities, hobbies and pastimes, cultural pursuits, and the list could go on and on!

Yet all of these things have a common factor—they show that we need to do things, we need to take actions, and we need to take control of our lives in a manner that will allow us to enjoy our daily lives and feel that joy (or happiness) that God intends for each of us. One of my dearest friends likes to say that there is no point in complaining, as it just means that he hasn't done enough to make things better. Each of us needs to realize that we need to take actions that will have a positive impact upon our lives, and that the moments when we make those decisions or choices can be moments that change our perspectives and our lives, and that those moments can define us for the rest of our lives. One of the clear Defining Moments of my life was what I like to call the *Day of My Awakening!*

On February 13, 1989, my father died. He had lived 61 years, 2 months, and 22 days on the day of his death. On November 18, 2016, I had lived 61 years, 2 months, and 22 days—that was the *day of my awakening.*

Reaching the same age as my father when he died did not come as a surprise. I am a list and numbers person and had this date circled on my calendar more than a year in advance. However, when I reached that ominous date it impacted me in a way I did not expect. For once in my life I didn't think about myself first but rather about my father.

Paul Liechty was a simple, hard-working man who provided for his family as best he could. He did not achieve great wealth—at least not in the sense it is commonly measured, but he was a man idolized and adored by his family and respected by everyone that knew him. He struggled with his own personal demons, as we all do, but managed to hold his world together, stay married to the same woman for thirty-nine years, and raise five children who have all lived productive lives, raised their own children, and contributed to their various communities. By any meaningful measure, my father had a very successful life.

Yet on the day I reached his age on his final day, I realized that his last few months were probably spent thinking about the same things I was thinking about on a daily basis. Things like working and making a living while transitioning into retirement; wanting to spend more time with his children and grandchildren; travelling to those select destinations that had always intrigued him; working in his church and community of faith; serving others; experiencing a few more adventures; and sharing life moments with dear friends. However, the sobering thought struck me that while I could still do those things, my father did not have those opportunities after reaching that age.

Suddenly, a light turned on. It struck me that every day I had after November 18, 2016, was an *extra day*, a day that my father never got to experience; every *extra day* was a gift from God that my father did not receive. Everything I could do after that day was something he didn't have the opportunity to do. More importantly, I realized that I had a choice. I could either live each of those days in the same manner that I had lived the previous 61 years, 2 months, and 22 days, or I could make each of those *extra days* into something special. That was an easy choice!

On the *day of my awakening*, I vowed to do everything possible to maximize each and every day thereafter. I recognized that I didn't want to simply chase experiences. I wanted to make my life full and complete and not just live in a manner to enhance small talk at cocktail parties. Rather than make a list of things to accomplish, I made a list of five activities that I really enjoyed and vowed to try and do something within each area of interest on that list each year.

Since the *day of my awakening* I have worked less, visited my children and grandchildren more, fallen more in love with my wife, taught small groups at our church, spoken at our grandchildren's school, volunteered at our local food pantry, and thoroughly enjoyed a family reunion. I have also begun wearing a gold chain, completed a triathlon, led a trip to

Israel with Mary, hunted moose, swam across the lake behind our home (more than two miles), ridden a motorcycle through Glacier National Park, set a new personal speed record in downhill skiing, acted in our local community theater, bought a convertible to be my daily driver, and expanded my book collection.

Frequently friends say something to me like, "Checked another item off your bucket list, huh?" I cringe at those comments because chasing checkmarks on a bucket list is not my goal. I am not checking off a finite list of things to do while waiting for my final day; rather, I like to think that on the *day of my awakening* I restarted my life with an infinite list of opportunities!

Like my father, someday I will pass from this earthly life to my heavenly reward. In my first 61 years, 2 months, and 22 days, I worked very hard and had a lot of success and achievements to go along with my share of disappointments and regrets; however, I am certain that I did not maximize all of those days. If I am fortunate and sentient enough to review my life on the day of my death, I hope to look back and say that at least I maximized my *extra days*.

CHAPTER 8

Micromoments

"A journey of a thousand miles begins with a single step."

—ANCIENT CHINESE PROVERB

The term "microaggression" was coined by Harvard University professor Chester M. Pierce in 1970 to describe insults and dismissals which he regularly witnessed nonblack Americans inflicting on African Americans.[1] The first time I heard the term I didn't get it—and I am certainly not alone in this.

What is particularly difficult about the concept is that the people committing microaggressions often fail to recognize them as such and don't even realize they have said or done something that has a negative impact on others. While the harm resulting from each microaggression may be described as a "microharm," the cumulative effect of multiple microaggressions becomes significant. Consequently, those microharms can eventually get to the point where they result in an eruption that can cause massive societal disruption, especially when a macroaggression serves as the spark. We saw that frequently in the United States with the protests in the summer of 2020 after the death of George Floyd in Minneapolis, Minnesota.

The concept of microaggressions correlates to our discussion of Defining Moments as well. We tend to view Defining Moments as major events or big moments in our lives—and that certainly often is the case.

However, in the course of our daily lives we are confronted with daily decisions and choices (micromoments) which standing alone may seem relatively insignificant; however, these micromoments build and accumulate, shaping the consequences of Defining Moments we encounter.

Just as the cumulative result of multiple microaggressions leading to a massive societal eruption, a series of micromoments can result in a major Defining Moment in our lives. We may not take time to recognize the micromoments in our lives, but they result in little decisions that lead to changes in our character, good or bad, which ultimately result in us becoming the people we are. Seemingly insignificant acts in those micromoments lead to habits; habits result in character traits; and character traits define who we are and are hard to change.

In this chapter we will look at the importance of those micromoments, how they can affect us, and what we can do to make sure that we respond effectively to them. We will also see how those micromoments can shape our decision-making when we are faced with larger and clearly recognizable Defining Moments.

LITTLE DECISIONS BECOME BIG DECISIONS

As any parent knows, raising children is one of the most difficult yet rewarding challenges we face in life. Each child is precious and you only get one opportunity to shape their character, so we all feel the pressure to get it right. Mary and I were blessed with four children. Like all parents, we struggled with each decision we had to make. It often seemed that everyone had an opinion on how to manage the process and that most of those opinions said I should be doing things differently!

As my children were growing up, I knew it was important to teach them to focus on the little decisions they faced each day if I wanted to shape their character. To make the point to them, I used a very simple phrase: Little decisions become big decisions. Each time they made a behavioral choice, they were shaping and defining their character—one little decision at a time.

Earlier in this book we said that a Defining Moment can be an achievement or a failure, something you do or something you go through; but you will know you have experienced a Defining Moment if you are a different person after you have been through it. If that is our standard it would seem unlikely that any single micromoment is likely to be a Defining Moment in a person's life. But when those micromoments are combined over a period of time, they can result in what cumulatively becomes a Defining Moment. In that manner, the little decisions arising from the micromoments can accumulate to become the Defining Moments in our lives.

This principle can apply to any area of our lives, but let's take the example of personal finances and I will continue using my children as an example. There are a lot of good ways to teach your children about managing their personal finances and many good resources available to parents today. I tried to always teach my children to save their money and to give to God (tithe). As they grew older and started working, I repeatedly used a simple principle. I told them that if they saved 10 percent of every paycheck they received, they would be able to retire young and in a relative sense, wealthy. The first time they made that decision to save 10 percent, it didn't look like much money had been set aside. However, as my children grew older, those small deposits (little decisions) accumulated into larger deposits (big decisions), and before long they saw the wisdom of Dad's advice.

Somehow in my childhood and through my teenage years, I became a very negative person with a very caustic wit. Criticism of others was a common weapon, and I developed an outlook that something bad was always just around the corner. This aspect of my personality must have been readily visible to others. Once in a high school English class I raised my hand to respond to a question and my teacher said, "Alright, let's hear from negative Lorne!"

I moved on to college and my attitude got worse. I loved college and all the new information I was learning. Like so many young people, however, that sudden influx of knowledge made me think I was smarter than I was and that I knew more than anyone else. That knowledge fed my caustic and sarcastic attitude and I became even more negative and probably miserable to live with. Everyone else was wrong, the institutions around me were all messed up, and there was little hope for our future unless our society experienced radical change—and I was willing to tell this to anyone who would listen. Still clinging to a bit of the faith I grew up with, some buddies of mine and I started CDSS—Christians for a Democratic Socialist Society—which was not well received on the campus of Oral Roberts University in the mid 1970s! I was sure the world would only improve if the hypocrisy of our institutions (in my case the school I attended) and our Christian religion was exposed.

Unlike me, my brother, Paul, chose a different approach. He saw the opportunities life had to offer and was excited about them. He realized that the world for him could be as great as he saw it. As he likes to say, "You live your whole life between your ears." He went to Palmer Chiropractic College and saw a vision of his future and wanted to make it happen. As you would expect, he had little time for negativism because the world he envisioned was a positive world where he could experience the fullness of life God has promised us. He was then and still is now the most optimistic and positive person I have ever known.

Paul and I have always been close, and we visited each other multiple times during our years of college and professional school. One time during my senior year at ORU, my brother came to visit for a long weekend. After he left, I realized what a striking difference there was between his positive outlook on life and my negative outlook. I realized that he embraced a future of great hope and promise, but I saw a future with little hope for achieving anything and only struggles and frustration to be dealt with on a daily basis. Thankfully, that weekend I realized that he was much happier in his positive view of the world than I was in my negative view, and I decided that his approach seemed the better of the two.

As a result, I decided I was going to change my outlook and become a more positive person. That weekend visit was definitely a Defining Moment in my life. However, as anyone who has tried to break from an addiction can tell you, making a decision to change, and changing, are two entirely different things. What I didn't realize at the time was that my negative attitude had become much like an addiction, and changing it was not something that would happen overnight. However, each time thereafter that I made a little decision to be positive in a micromoment, it changed my character in a positive way. In that way, that Defining Moment was really the commencement of a refining process in me. That refining process coupled with God's grace is what converts our micromoments into character changing Defining Moments.

Eventually all my daily little decisions brought to fruition the big decision I had made after that weekend at college and the promise of that Defining Moment was ultimately fulfilled in my life. Yet even today, forty-five years later, I still have moments when my old negative nature bursts out. When that happens, I invariably am frustrated, realize that the old Lorne has reappeared, and renew my vow of that Defining Moment to be more positive in the future.

BAD MICROCHOICES CAN DESTROY LIVES

Developing a more positive attitude took years and led me to a better life. On the contrary, however, the pages of history are full of bad decisions leading to damaged reputations, financial ruin, and ultimately, destroyed lives. I am convinced that many of those stories we hear about are the conclusions that result from a series of bad choices made in the micromoments that shape our character. The little choices we make that may seem insignificant at the time can lead to big choices and unanticipated consequences that were never imagined when facing the micromoments.

If you work as an attorney long enough, you get to see just about everything. In the late 1980s my professional career led me into direct involvement in the savings and loan business in Texas, first as an attorney for a savings and loan association, and then with the FADA, the federal agency charged with cleaning up the financial disaster arising from years of high-risk loans, changing tax laws, lack of adequate appraisal standards, and in some cases outright fraud.

As I went through that phase of my career, I saw many instances where men with otherwise stellar business careers ended up in the crosshairs of government agencies seeking to recover lost assets of the savings and loans, or, in the most egregious cases, to put them in prison. In several cases I knew the people who were being sued or prosecuted by the government, and in a few instances even had to testify in their trials.

Despite the sometimes desperate situations these men got themselves into, I never saw a single instance where people made conscious decisions at the outset of their careers to commit fraud. On the contrary, in most cases these were decent people, classic good guys who just started taking high risks, pushing the envelope, and assuming nothing would happen from the decisions they made. Often in those micromoments nothing did happen, which eased their anxiety the next time they were faced with a making an ethically questionable decision. And ultimately they made a decision that pushed the envelope a bit too far, came under scrutiny, and ruined their finances, careers, and sometimes their families—and typically they never saw it coming.

There are innumerable stories of bad choices in micromoments leading to a ruined life, and they appear in all professions and walks of life. In chapter 3 we discussed the life of Samson in the context of God giving second chances. Yet his life is an equally good example of the principle of micromoments discussed in this chapter. Samson repeatedly made bad decisions in micromoments and always seemed to get away with it—until he didn't, and paid the price of destroying his life.

In the modern world we have also seen this principle played out multiple times, often on a global stage, and with our instant communications, ruined lives are displayed on our computer and television screens for everyone to see.

- In the world of finance, Bernie Madoff seemed to be an incredibly successful stock trader and financier, rising to the position of chairman of the NASDAQ stock market, until it was revealed that his career had been built on a series of fraudulent trading schemes that started small, continued for decades, and became the largest Ponzi scheme in world history and the largest financial fraud in U.S. history.[2]

- In sports, Pete Rose was one of the greatest baseball players in history, retiring from major league baseball as the all-time leader in hits and several other statistical categories. Yet he fell from grace amid allegations that he bet on baseball, to which he ultimately confessed. Equally sad is the story of Lance Armstrong, who may have been the greatest cyclist of all time but whose reputation was destroyed when it was revealed that he used banned performance-enhancing substances for many years.

- In politics, President Bill Clinton's career and his otherwise successful presidency were forever tarnished when it was revealed that he had engaged in sexual relations with a White House intern and he perjured himself.

- And even in the arena of faith, there are multiple examples of scandal that are too sad to recite. Pastors, priests, and church leaders whose lives and ministries have been destroyed by sin that they thought could be hidden, even though the Bible they studied and preached told them that what they did and said in secret would be shouted from the housetops.[3]

We should all learn from our mistakes, but it is much less painful to learn from the mistakes of others. All of these examples and others should be reminders to us of the need to walk in integrity in all that we do, even in those micromoments. Indeed, white lies are still lies, and while our God is a God of limitless grace, there are consequences to our actions. The little decisions made in those micromoments may ultimately become the big decisions that destroy a life.

YOU WANT TO CHANGE—NOW WHAT?

I'm not trained as a sociologist or psychologist, but I feel comfortable making the conclusory statement that we all have things in our lives that we want to change for the better. Sometimes they are small things, like losing a few extra pounds; and sometimes they are major things, like learning a new skill, earning another degree, or finding a spouse. But in each case they are things we want, and even though we may be convinced of the value of achieving these goals, we find that we are challenged by the difficulty of such achievements. Further, we struggle with the seeming dichotomy that the difficulty of achieving our personal goals and objectives seems to increase in direct proportion to the importance we place on those goals.

That dichotomy is easily explained, however, when we realize that our more-important goals require more work to achieve. Accomplishing big goals takes a lot of time and a long-term commitment. Sounds obvious, right? Yet even though we all know that, we all want things to happen quickly. Part of the reason we struggle with this is that we see many examples of success but don't often hear about the time and effort required to reach that success.

Not surprisingly (or surprisingly?), the difficulty of achieving goals is not automatically reduced by becoming a Christian. In fact, at the risk of sounding heretical, sometimes the path to achieving goals might seem to be even more difficult after becoming a Christian. I think this is at least partially because the salvation experience is such a life-changing experience in itself that we expect instant changes, instant resolution of our bad habits, etc., as a result of becoming a believer. We are told that our lives will be changed forever but are not always told that our entire life doesn't necessarily change overnight. We still will need to deal with character issues that have developed over the course of our life. For example, if we have spent a lifetime being lazy, becoming a Christian won't make us wake up early the next morning as a diligent and hard-working person.

In fact, even as we read the Bible we see many stories of what seem like instantaneous change and overnight successes, which may make us think we can expect the same results. (You might even say that the Bible is a book which focuses on stories of Defining Moments!) However, what we should recognize is that the rewards promised in the Bible are frequently the result of the character changes that result in our lives from putting in the hard work and effort to live a godly life. The refining process, coupled with God's grace, is what brings these promised results.

For example, we all love the story of David's victory over the giant, Goliath—small, young boy straight from watching his father's sheep wins a great victory and becomes a national hero despite the fact that he was outmatched by a gigantic man who also happens to be a trained warrior. It almost makes you want to go grab a slingshot and take on the world! However, the story behind what made that victory possible is hidden within the text of the story itself in 1 Samuel 17. By studying this passage, we see that David had developed his character to fight for what is a right and noble cause;[4] that he had learned to be willing to put his life on the line to fulfill his duties of protecting the sheep entrusted to him;[5] and that he had worked to become skillful with a sling, the weapon he chose to fight against Goliath.[6] Those characteristics and abilities all took time to develop and were necessary to achieve David's victory over the giant he faced.

Similarly, we must invest the necessary time and effort if we want to realize the changes we desire in our lives. There are many formulas and descriptions of how to accomplish personal change, but ultimately it takes a force of will with God's help for those changes to develop and for those little decisions to mature into big decisions. Here are some ideas that will help:

1. *Set Specific Goals.* Hall of Fame baseball player and pop culture philosopher Yogi Berra said, "If you don't know where you are going, you might wind up someplace else." If you want to achieve something, set your goal and be specific about it. Only then will you know the target you are shooting for.

2. *Map Out a Path to Achieve Your Goals.* After you have set your goal, take the time to figure out what it will take to get you there. Unless you do that, you will easily be discouraged when instant success is absent.

3. *Eliminate Distractions.* We live in a world of so many options that we have a hard time focusing on what is important. We might make ourselves feel good by saying that we are multitasking but often we are just being distracted from our purpose. We need to acknowledge that we have set a priority to accomplish something and then eliminate other things (which in and of themselves may not be bad things) in our lives that hinder, distract, and prevent us from reaching that goal.

4. *Pay the Price.* Nothing really valuable is accomplished easily. Even those fortunate people who are truly gifted in an area of life need to work hard to maximize those gifts. If that is the case, those of us who often feel we struggle to achieve the status of average need to work all the harder.

Our youngest son, Harley, was ten years younger than his nearest sibling and consequently grew up almost like an only child. He was always an exceptionally confident child, but sometimes that confidence exploded into bravado, and often bravado without a basis in preparation or practice. When he was young that was a fun part of his persona. However, as he grew older I worried more and more whether he would have the persistence and intestinal fortitude it takes to accomplish meaningful goals in his life. He seemed much too willing to post what he *was going to do* on Facebook before he *actually did it*!

One Christmas, sometime during his early twenties, Harley told me that he wanted to become a good jazz pianist within five years and explained to me how much and often he would have to practice to accomplish that. I wished him well but inside remembered some of the other dreams he had cast that never came to fruition.

However, this time it was different. Harley had recently taken a job with a business-consulting firm in Tulsa, Oklahoma, that demanded results. They had taught him not only to set goals, but also to monitor progress, make corrections as necessary, and expect results. Harley adopted these policies and implemented them toward accomplishing his personal goal. Consistent with the recommendations specified above, he (1) Set a Specific Goal, to be a good jazz pianist (which he defined as being capable of competently performing before other people) within five years; (2) Mapped Out a Plan to Achieve this Goal, which required finding a good teacher and setting specific weekly practice requirements; (3) Eliminated Distractions, by getting rid of other activities that were cluttering his life; and (4) Paid the Price, by scheduling lessons and practicing regularly. In fact, to increase his dedication to piano, he even got a part-time job as a piano teacher.

Harley also loves producing music and with some friends recently recorded and produced a jazz album featuring himself on the piano.

He is not yet as accomplished a pianist as he wants to become, but he's getting there. More importantly, wherever his dream takes him, Harley has already accomplished something much more valuable. He has learned the importance of self-discipline in his daily micromoments and has incorporated that self-discipline into his life. With that skill he can do anything!

CHAPTER 9

Butterflies, Ripples on a Pond, and Neighbors

"No man is an island entire of itself . . . ."

—JOHN DONNE

The 139th meeting of the American Association for the Advancement of Science, held in December 1972, was not a meeting that would be expected to attract much public attention outside of the small group of scientists and academics who attended. In fact, my guess is that no one reading this book has ever heard of that meeting before. However, at that meeting, Edward N. Lorenz, ScD, a Professor of Meteorology at the Massachusetts Institute of Technology, submitted a paper with the title, "Does the Flap of a Butterfly's Wings in Brazil Set Off a Tornado in Texas?" and that subject title has caught on in our pop culture.[1]

Commonly referred to as *The Butterfly Effect,* the term is used loosely to emphasize that even a miniscule act can have consequences which can be significant and are impossible to predict with accuracy. Dr. Lorenz proposed that the most such miniscule disturbances can do is to modify the sequence in which weather events such as tornados may occur, but that the randomness of such miniscule disturbances made weather forecasting an inexact science, at best. However, the possibility that such a miniscule event may affect more significant weather events, and especially in faraway locations, raises a plethora of possibilities that are engaging to imagine and lays the basis for our minds to consider an endless number of possible story lines.

The Butterfly Effect is relevant to our discussion of Defining Moments. To this point we have been discussing and analyzing the impact of Defining Moments on our own lives. However, as Christians we must recognize that we don't live our lives solely for ourselves. In fact, one of the central themes of the Bible is our many obligations to others. We are taught to serve others, give unto others, risk our lives for others, and subordinate our desires to the greater good of our families and our Christian communities.

Therefore, it is essential that our study of Defining Moments includes a consideration of the impact upon others of the decisions we make in the Defining Moments of our lives. I think we will see that unlike the chaos and randomness surrounding the impact of a butterfly flapping its wings in Brazil, we will be able to see relatively direct effects of our actions on others. This in turn requires that our *analysis* of Defining Moments—the second element of our RARE equation—must include the impact of our decisions on our families, our Christian community, our neighbors, and to an extent, society as a whole.

RECOGNIZING OUR RESPONSIBILITY

To say we live in a selfish world is a gross understatement. Everywhere we turn, it seems the narcissism of the *Me Generation* (a term often used to describe the Baby Boomers' generation) has gone out of control. The cover of *Time* magazine's May 20, 2013, edition recognized this point with its story, "The Me Me Me Generation." The *Monitor on Psychology,* published by the American Psychological Association, asked its readers to imagine a country where everyone acts like a reality show contestant—obsessed with power, status, and appearance, and is comfortable manipulating others for their personal gain. It would be a society where cosmetic surgery would be routine, materialism rampant, and everyone would seek fame or notoriety. The article quoted Christopher Barry, PhD, as saying, "A narcissistic society would be a deeply lonely place."[2] Unfortunately, when we consider our world today it seems that we are either living in that world or headed that way—or even more concerning, we are even past that stage and are experiencing a new level of narcissism that we have not yet taken the time to identify and define!

Even more concerning is that our churches and the American Christian community seem to be headed in the same direction. But that is not what God called us to be! We are called to be the salt of the earth and the light of the world.[3] We are called to love our neighbors as ourselves.[4] If that is our goal and our calling, we need to consider how our decisions affect others. When we are facing our most important decisions, those made in the Defining Moments of our lives, we especially need to consider the impact of our actions on those around us. The decisions made in those moments not only affect us, but they also affect others, especially those closest to us and most dependent upon us. If we make our decisions thinking only about what's in it for me, we are missing one of the most central points of the gospel and are likely to do harm, and often significant harm, to those around us. And sadly, like waves rippling from a rock thrown into a pond, the impact of our actions is most significant on those that are closest to us.

John the Baptist was an amazing person. For starters, his birth and his ministry were foretold by the angel Gabriel,[5] and that alone puts him in pretty elite company! While his exact relationship to Christ is not specified in the Bible, Mary, the Mother of Christ, was a relative of John's mother, Elizabeth,[6] and it is commonly assumed they were cousins of some degree. So based upon that relationship, John the Baptist was likely a distant cousin of Christ.

It was foretold that he would go before Christ in the spirit and power of Elijah and would turn many of the children of Israel to the Lord their God.[7] Upon his birth, John's father, Zacharias the priest, prophesied that John would be called a prophet of God, that he would give knowledge of salvation to God's people, and would give light to those who sat in darkness.[8] From these verses it is obvious that John had a critical calling on his life. The Bible doesn't say much about John's childhood but does tell us that he grew and became strong in the spirit. We can assume that his parents, who were godly people, raised him to understand the Scriptures and prepared him for his calling.

As John reached maturity, he began to fulfill his calling, preaching a baptism of repentance from sins. From the scriptural accounts, it appears that John's ministry was extremely successful. In Luke chapter 3, it says that multitudes came out to be baptized by him. Also, it appears that he reached out to many of the same people that Christ reached out to, as tax collectors and soldiers came out to see him.

We can speculate about what it was like to be around John the Baptist at that time, but it is likely that it was an electric atmosphere. In today's world he would likely be viewed as an extremely successful minister—maybe a successful televangelist or megachurch pastor in our time! He apparently even had been noticed by and possibly had access to the leading political figure of the day, King Herod. He had a successful ministry, he was well known, and people were flocking to hear him. The temptation to let all this go to your head would be immense, and one thing that makes John such an amazing character is that he didn't let that happen.

Rather than fawning before the king or seeking to take advantage of his access to him, he confronted the king and his sinful state. Rather than seek favor with the religious leaders of his day, he called them (the Sadducees and Pharisees) a brood of vipers and commanded that they repent.

And at this point, John the Baptist faces his Defining Moment. Here he is, at the peak of his ministry. People are flocking to hear him. He has attracted the attention of the political and religious leaders of his day. His success had reached a point that people were asking whether or not he was the Christ! Unfortunately, we tend to not recognize the significance of John's answer to the multitudes. Think about the situation he was in. He had everyone's attention—he was a rock star! If he would have claimed to be the Christ, many would have probably believed him and he could have kept his ministry alive. However, John recognized his limited role and said, "I am not the Christ," and that, "He (Christ) must increase but I (John) must decrease."[9]

In doing that, John subordinates his ministry to the ministry of Christ. He recognizes that he is not to be the center of attention and that Jesus, his younger cousin, is to be the focus of everyone's attention. By his answer he turns everyone's attention to Jesus, as the multitudes now follow after Christ. John, on the other hand, sees his ministry decline and goes on to experience a vicious and lonely death by being beheaded.[10] In that Defining Moment, John recognized the situation and the importance of his answer. By responding effectively, he impacted many who turned from his ministry and followed Christ, and John did so even though the consequences to him were devastating—at least from an earthly perspective. John recognized his responsibility and acted appropriately despite the consequences to him personally. Would we be willing to do the same?

WHO IS YOUR NEIGHBOR?

The story of the good Samaritan is one of the most challenging parables in the Bible.[11] The preface to the parable is that an expert in the law came to Christ asking what he needed to do to obtain eternal life. Christ replied, as He often did, with a question: "What is written in the

Law? How do you read it?" The lawyer's reply, "Love the Lord your God with all your heart and with all your soul and with all your strength and with all you mind, and love your neighbor as yourself," was perfect, and Jesus replied, "You have answered correctly, do this and you will live."

At that point the lawyer should have been satisfied. Think of it; Jesus Christ, the Son of God, just said that you gave the right answer! No greater imprimatur could have been asked or received. At this point he could have quit and been quite satisfied with himself. However, the Bible says that wasn't enough for him, and that seeking to justify himself, he asked, "And who is my neighbor?" One of the things they teach you in law school is to never ask a witness a question unless you already know the answer. I am so glad that the lawyer in this biblical story did not adhere to that principle because had he done so, we might not have received the parable of the good Samaritan.

You probably know the story, but if you don't, please read it. The short version is that a traveler was attacked by robbers and left to die. Two men, a priest and a Levite (a person charged with caring for the temple and leading worship) passed by the beaten and abused man but left him in the roadway without helping him. A Samaritan (a person despised by the Jews at that time) came upon the man and took pity on him. The Samaritan bandaged his wounds, took the man to an inn, and promised to pay the costs incurred by the innkeeper in caring for the wounded man. Jesus then asked the lawyer, "Which of these three do you think was a neighbor to the man who fell into the hands of robbers?" The lawyer answered, "The one who had mercy on him." Jesus looked him in the eyes (please excuse the license taken here) and said, "Go and do likewise." And with that charge we are each given the responsibility to help everyone that we can.

So how does this apply to our study of Defining Moments? As described above, the decisions we make in our Defining Moments affect and impact others. The description of our neighbors in this parable requires us to consider the expansive reach of decisions made in our

Defining Moments. If the decisions we are making affect others, those others can be considered our neighbors. We need to think about how our decisions made in our Defining Moments affect them and consider those effects when we make our decisions. We have previously considered Defining Moments in our personal, professional, and spiritual lives. Now let's think for a bit about how the decisions in those situations affect others—remembering that the descriptions in this section do not address all situations.

1. *Personal Defining Moments.* The decisions we make in our personal life have an incredible impact upon the people closest to us. As an example, consider the impact of divorce upon your spouse and your children. Thoughts of, *What is best for me?* or *How is he/she negatively impacting my life?* cannot be considered more important than the related questions of, *How will this impact my spouse, the person I pledged myself to?* or *How will this affect my children, the people I brought into this world?* Our narcissistic world minimizes the impact of our decisions on others. However, if our spouse and our children are not our neighbors, no one is.

2. *Professional Defining Moments.* The world we live in tells us to maximize our careers, and to an extent, that is consistent with Scripture. However, decisions we make in advancing our careers can impact others, and we must consider that when making those decisions. On a recent trip, we spent the night in one location of a well-known national hotel chain. It quickly became apparent to my wife and me that this location was well below the national organization's standards. When talking with the lady at the front desk (who was quickly reduced to tears), my wife learned that shortly after she had been hired, both her immediate supervisor and that supervisor's supervisor had quit and left her to run the hotel. No manager had been in place for two weeks, and she was ready to quit her first, and possibly last, job in the hospitality

industry. The decisions those supervisors made to hire her and then quit had a huge impact on her life. Similarly, career advancement often involves moving to another city. How will that affect your spouse and your children, and what will be the result on them of the consequent disruption of their worlds? Whether considering our families, coworkers, or other neighbors, we need to deal with others with integrity and fairness, even if that impacts our own lives.

3. *Spiritual Defining Moments.* So often we tend to think that the decisions we make regarding our spiritual lives affect only us. Nothing could be further from the truth. Some of the most significant relationships we make in our lives are our relationships with other believers. If God called you to attend a specific church, He called you into relationship with others at that church. If you choose to leave, you will impact others, and possibly their faith. In the book of 1 Corinthians, Paul addresses this when he says, "If food makes my brother stumble, I will never again eat meat, lest I make my brother stumble."[12] Consider the impact decisions made in your spiritual life may have on others rather than making those decisions solely based on what is best for you.

In 1981, Mary and I began attending Church on the Rock in Rockwall, Texas. That church had a massive impact on our lives and helped draw us closer to the Lord early in our married life. We were brought into a community of believers that emphasized prayer, praise, and Christian community. We participated in ministry at the church. Our children attended the church's school and were taught the faith in a way that had a positive impact upon them.

The church grew rapidly and quickly became one of the first national megachurches. There were four locations in the Dallas-Fort Worth metroplex and other affiliated churches were formed around the country and internationally. National figures would show up to speak in tiny Rockwall, Texas, and it seemed like the church was destined to have a great impact on the world for the Kingdom of God. We loved our pastor, and he loved the church and its people. He frequently made references that God had called him there to lead our congregation. I couldn't imagine a better church situation for us at that time, and thousands of others felt the same way.

However, after we had been attending there for about ten years, the original pastor's ministry expanded and the church brought in a new senior pastor. Although our original pastor was to remain involved in the church, the relationship between the two pastors (original and successor) deteriorated, and soon the original pastor was no longer allowed to speak in the church he had started. As you would expect, factions developed within the church, and the group siding with our original pastor was no longer happy. Within five years, thousands had left our church, causing the church to dwindle. The reduction in the size of the congregation led to a reduction in giving. Unfortunately, a large bond issue had been used to generate funds to build the church's main building. The church was unable to make the bond payments and ultimately declared bankruptcy and moved to another city. Today it continues to operate under another name and with a much smaller congregation.

It pains me to write that story because I still love our pastors, both the original visionary and his successor. Further, it hurts to recognize that many of the people that left the church were never able to find another church that ministered to their needs as Church on the Rock had done. Relationships were damaged, and people drifted away.

This story illustrates the impact that decisions made in our Defining Moments can have on others. In this case, the original pastor felt he was being called to another ministry and left his role as senior pastor to pursue it. The new pastor was convinced that he was leading the church into a new direction and told those who did not share his vision that they could vote with their feet—and they did. Thousands of people were impacted by those decisions, and a ministry that seemed destined for a worldwide impact shriveled to a footnote in church history.

I cannot blame those pastors alone for decisions made by many people to leave our church and the negative consequences that flowed from those decisions. As individuals, we are all responsible for our own decisions. However, I can't help but believe that if the founding senior pastor had remained and stayed true to his vision for our church or if the new pastor had worked in harmony with him that many of those who left would have stayed, and the impact of Church on the Rock would have been much greater than it is today. Who is my neighbor? Those who rely upon me and trust in me certainly fall within that definition.

GOD'S WILL DOES NOT RECOGNIZE MIRROR UNIVERSES

The TV series *Star Trek* has captured the imagination of multiple generations. Despite the fact that the original series only lasted three seasons on network television, the concept generated multiple movies and additional television series. *Star Trek* has achieved cult status, as generations of Trekkies, casual viewers, and even those who may have never watched the shows recognize the *Enterprise* and Mr. Spock, and use terms like "Beam me aboard, Scottie" and "travel at warp speed" in daily conversations. In fact, if you do an internet search you will find multiple articles talking about ways in which *Star Trek* predicted the future or influenced scientific development.

One of the episodes of the original *Star Trek* series, titled "Mirror, Mirror," presents the intriguing concept of a transporter malfunction causing Captain Kirk and three other crew members to be sent to a different version of the starship *Enterprise*, where Mr. Spock and the rest of the crew behave completely different, and where torture and murder are commonplace and accepted as a method of discipline and conquest.

It turns out that Kirk and his three crew members have been transported into a mirror universe, and that the Captain Kirk and crew members from that alternate universe have been transported onto the *Enterprise* that viewers were familiar with. For those who enjoy science fiction and stories involving time travel and alternate realities, it is a fascinating episode and has been rated as one of the best of the original series.

The concept of parallel universes introduced in the "Mirror, Mirror" episode can lead to interesting dinner table conversations. However, it is important to recognize that no such concept applies with respect to God's will for us when we are facing Defining Moments. In fact, just the opposite. In the *Star Trek* story, the actions taken by the characters in one universe did not affect the counterpart crew members in the other universe. However, like the ripples made when a rock is thrown into a smooth pond or the movement of wind when a butterfly flaps its wings, the decisions we make when faced with Defining Moments affect people within our circles of influence, and the closer they are to us, the more they are impacted by our decisions. We cannot make our decisions as though others are living in a parallel universe and are unaffected by our actions!

When we face our Defining Moments, we need to realize that the decisions we are making will have an impact on others around us. If we are seeking to make decisions that fulfill God's will in our lives, we need to recognize that those decisions must be consistent with God's will for the other people affected by those decisions. In other words, if I think an action I am about to take is God's will for my life, then my taking that action and the consequences rippling from that action must be consistent with God's will for others affected by it.

Looking at our decisions in this way will lead us to strip away the selfishness that often is the basis for our actions. Viewing our decisions this way is not only consistent with biblical principles, but it will also lead those around us into God's will for their lives and allow them to enjoy the blessing that God pours out on us when we walk in His will.

Years ago, while interviewing an attorney for a job in our office, he mentioned that he was a Christian and was looking to go where God wanted him to go. He had been through a couple of job changes but had not found the right place for himself. At the time, my law partner told him that if it was God's will for us to hire him, then it would also be God's will for him to come to work for us. God's will would be consistent for both of us. That interview was nearly twenty years ago. We hired that attorney, he stayed with us, and he eventually became a partner in our firm. In doing so, he has found the role in his professional life that was meant for him and has been blessed, both financially and professionally, more than ever before and more than he had ever imagined. Similarly, he has been a blessing to our firm and allowed us to grow and expand our business. It has been rewarding to watch such consistency manifested through God's will in his life and in ours.

We need to recognize that God's will for one person's life is consistent with His will for those impacted by that first person. God's will is not a zero-sum game, where each party struggles to grab their own piece of the pie and the cumulative losses and wins add up to a net of zero. Rather, when we all flow in God's will, we move together. Our net gains and losses are cumulatively greater than zero as we get to share the blessings of others walking with us on the highway to heaven.

Earlier in this chapter we pointed out how John the Baptist recognized his role and his responsibility to point others to Christ, even going to the point of saying that He (Christ) must increase but I (John) must decrease.[13] But the impact of John pointing others to Christ and the consistency of God's will for John and those around him is clearly evident by the impact it had on two of Christ's twelve disciples.

The first chapter of the book of John describes how John the Baptist prepared the way for Christ.[14] The Bible mentions that John the Baptist had disciples of his own, but when he was walking with two of them, he said, "Behold the Lamb of God!" By saying this, coupled with his prior comments preparing the way for Christ, John effectively was telling those two disciples of his to follow Christ, and that is exactly what they did. One of those two disciples of John was Andrew, and he went and called his brother Peter to go with him. Thus, the rock upon whom Christ would build His Church became a disciple of Jesus.[15]

We could speculate about what would have happened if John the Baptist had not responded as he did in that Defining Moment in his life. For example, would Andrew have stayed a disciple of John rather than becoming a disciple of Christ?[16] Would Andrew have called his brother, Peter, to join him in following John rather than Christ? However, God's will doesn't recognize parallel universes. It was God's will for John that he should decrease and Christ increase, and that was perfectly consistent with God's will for John's disciple, Andrew, and his brother, Peter. The results of that consistency and John's recognition of it established the foundation for the Christian Church over the past 2,000 years. Indeed, no man is an island.

CHAPTER 10

Define Your Future

"Now that you know these things, you will be blessed if you do them."

—John 13:17 (NIV)

Americans are fascinated with personal success stories, especially stories about individuals who pull themselves up by their own bootstraps. One of the most interesting American success stories is that of Colonel Harland David Sanders, and indeed, his story provides hope to all of us who are wondering about our own futures.

Harland Sanders was born on a farm near Henryville, Indiana, in 1890. His life was anything but easy. His father died when Sanders was only five years old, and he began helping his mother take care of his younger brother and sister. He was given responsibility for cooking and grew to enjoy it. His mother remarried, but his stepfather was harsh and literally threw him out of the house at the age of twelve.

His formal education ended after the sixth grade, but his education in the School of Hard Knocks continued. After being thrown out of the house, he worked several years for a farmer in Indiana. At age sixteen, about the time the United States was getting ready to enter World War I, he lied about his age, joined the army, and served in Cuba. After being discharged from the army, he worked on the railroad as a ferryboat operator, a streetcar conductor, and other miscellaneous jobs.

In 1930, at age forty and in the depths of the Great Depression, Sanders began running a small service station in Kentucky. He served food to hungry travelers, and his fried chicken was so good that Kentucky Governor Ruby Laffoon gave him the honorary title of being a Kentucky Colonel. At this point everything seemed to be going well for Colonel Sanders. However, if things had just continued going well for him, the fame of Kentucky Fried Chicken may never have spread around the world.

The 1950s brought the beginning of the Interstate Highway System in the United States. Although this was great for America, a newly constructed interstate highway reduced traffic on the road that went by Colonel Sanders' restaurant. For many people, the new highway system sounded the death knell for their businesses and their dreams. In fact, even today when driving across the United States you can see empty buildings on roadsides that used to be bustling places of business.

While many of the people running those small businesses were likely displaced, Colonel Sanders saw his failing business as a challenge. Despite the fact that he was at (or past) retirement age, Colonel Sanders *recognized* that this was a critical point in his professional career (*e.g.*, a Defining Moment), *analyzed* the situation, and *responded effectively* by deciding that this was an opportunity for him to capitalize on the experience he had been accumulating all his life. At age sixty-five he sold his one store on the then lightly travelled highway, and at age sixty-six began selling franchises, allowing others to sell his tasty Kentucky Fried Chicken.

His first franchisee was a businessman in Salt Lake City, Utah. His second franchisee was in Canada. Soon Colonel Sanders' life was changed forever. His business prospered and in 1964, with more than 600 franchised outlets, he sold his interest in the business for $2,000,000. He continued working for the company as a spokesperson into his eighties and became an iconic figure in the process. His distinctive white mustache and goatee were so familiar that at one point in his eighties, Colonel Sanders' image was said to be recognized by 97 percent of people in North America.[1]

While the success story of Colonel Sanders and Kentucky Fried Chicken is fascinating, equally amazing is how the Colonel handled his success. He knew that his was a God-given opportunity, and he promised God that if the business made good, God would get His share. Unlike many people making promises to God, the Colonel remained true to his word. Colonel Sanders' first tithe from his new business was $50,000, and he continued giving, eventually giving his entire Canadian operations to a charitable foundation.[2] He freely testified of his commitment to Christ and spoke of the importance of biblical values and virtues in business. Colonel Sanders thoroughly enjoyed his life and lived it to fulfill his purpose. In this, he is an example to all of us. When we are confronted with Defining Moments in our lives, at any age and in any circumstances, we need to respond in a way that will maximize the opportunities that are set before us and revel in fulfilling God's purpose for our lives.

"Today is the first day of the rest of your life" is a familiar quote attributed to Charles Dederich,[3] the founder of the Synanon drug rehabilitation program. We cannot reverse our actions or inaction regarding Defining Moments in our past, but we can determine that as we move forward we are going to work to maximize the results from future Defining Moments, whether great or small. To do that we need to be deliberate about our actions and plan for facing those Defining Moments as they arrive. This book has provided a lot of information about Defining Moments in our lives. As we near the conclusion, we will refocus on steps we need to take to put that information into practice.

REALIZE YOUR PURPOSE

Our purpose in life is not just to drift along and enjoy whatever comes our way. On the contrary, God has a plan for each of us, and each of us has a purpose to fulfill on this earth![4] Let that sink in for a minute. You were created with a purpose to fulfill. If you don't believe that, you will not maximize the consequences of your Defining Moments. However, if you accept and believe that you have a God-given purpose, you will realize the importance of the decisions you make in your Defining Moments, both at major life points and in the micromoments we encounter on a daily basis.

If you believe that you have been called for a specific purpose in life, it will affect decisions you make at every level. For example, if you believe you are called to serve as an agent in the FBI, you will need to pursue the education required to be accepted into that elite group of men and women. With just a minimal amount of research, you will learn that there are age, education, fitness, and other requirements to be an FBI agent.[5] Armed with that information, you will be able to make decisions effectively. A bachelor's degree from a U.S.-accredited college or university is mandatory, so you would need to enroll in a college or university that will satisfy that requirement. However, equally significant, you will realize that your daily decisions can affect the likelihood that you will be accepted for such a position. Those daily decisions will likely steer you away from illegal drug use, association with known criminals, and other things that would be viewed negatively in pursuing that position, and will make you pursue an exercise and physical fitness regimen that will allow you to meet the physical fitness standards of the FBI.

This all seems obvious. However, missing the obvious seems to happen regularly to people in our world. Realizing our purpose and keeping a daily focus on it will hopefully help us to recognize our Defining Moments, including micromoments, and let us achieve those objectives. It is important to keep those objectives at the forefront of our lives. This can be done by pictures or posters on our walls, accountability partners, study groups, and other methods, but the important thing is to not lose sight of that purpose!

I love magicians and watching them do their magic. Great magicians not only are able to perform their tricks, but they are also able to connect with the audience in a way that makes us feel that we are part of the show. I recently had the opportunity to watch a great young magician, Brice Harney, at work. I was fascinated by his magic tricks. However, I learned about the Defining Moments that changed his life when I spoke with him after the show. Brice's story is a great example of the need to realize your purpose and keep your hopes and dreams fixed on it.

Brice Harney was nine years old when he first saw David Blaine on television and was instantly mystified. The moment Blaine would complete a trick, his audience would react in amazement, and Brice wanted the same ability to bend reality and create an emotional experience for his audience with nothing more than a deck of cards or a borrowed dollar bill. Brice begged his parents for help to learn the secrets of those amazing feats, and for his tenth birthday present they gave him lessons with a professional magician. From then on, magic was all he could think about. Night after night he would sit in his room and practice, and the next day would test his prowess on his classmates during lunch.

By the time he was in high school, Brice started to show real talent for the art of magic and told his parents he wanted to be a professional magician. His parents, showing true wisdom, supported him but told him he needed to go to college, just in case magic didn't work out. Prior to this, Brice wasn't considering a college education, but in what turned out to be a Defining Moment for him, he decided to honor his parents and pursue a college degree.

Brice went to school at Western Kentucky University. His best friend had chosen WKU and Brice went along to study video production. While this choice may have seemed a bit haphazard at the time, in retrospect it is clear that God was leading him there. Attending WKU set the course for the next and most significant Defining Moment to this point in his life.

During his freshman year at WKU, Brice saw a notice for a magic show on campus called *Maze* and immediately made plans to attend. On the night of the show, he got to the theater early and sat in the front row. After an hour of mind-blowing tricks, the performer came back from intermission to share more magic along with a deeply personal story of his battle with cancer and his journey into Christian faith through his struggles. At the end of the show, he offered the opportunity for those in the audience to start their journey of faith by joining a campus ministry at WKU.

Brice was moved by the incredible performance *Maze* brought that night—not just by the magic, but also the message of how this man's faith carried him through the most difficult time of his life. Further, by watching that show Brice recognized that there was an avenue for him to fulfill his dream to be a professional magician. This was a Defining Moment in Brice's life, and he recognized it and knew he had to take advantage of the opportunity it presented.

After the show, Brice approached the performer and introduced himself and asked, "How do I do what you are doing? How do I become a professional magician?" The magician told him that *Maze* might have a spot open on their traveling team after he graduated and encouraged him to stay in contact, and again, to get involved with one of the ministries on campus.

In his excitement, Brice was ready to drop out of school that night and join *Maze*. However, he also recognized that would be inconsistent with the decision he had made to honor his parents' request to earn a college degree. Over the next three years of school, Brice followed the performer's advice and continued honing his magic skills and joined a campus ministry. By doing so, he learned how magic could intersect with faith, and his life was changed forever.

Brice learned that *Maze* was more than just a magic show. More significantly, it was a tool for evangelism that brought the message of Christ to millions across the country and around the world. Brice was one of the students affected by this ministry, and it provided him a path to fulfill his purpose in both his spiritual life and his professional life. Upon graduation, Brice was offered a spot on the *Maze* team and was on the path to becoming a professional magician. During the next four years touring the country with *Maze*, Brice learned how to be an entertainer and an evangelist. During that time Brice was given the opportunity to become the lead performer of *Maze*, which had become one of the most successful tools for evangelistic entertainment for the largest campus ministry in the world, Cru. He led a team, just like the one that came to WKU, sharing amazing magic along with the message of the gospel that had changed his life.

Brice handled his Defining Moment well, and the results have been—magical! In addition to allowing him to live his childhood dream and enjoy a fulfilled life in Christ, his affiliation with *Maze* also led him to meet the woman who became his wife. Brice has now started his own ministry, Nexus Outreach, sharing the message of Christ across the country through magic shows. However, none of that would have happened if Brice had not recognized his purpose and kept that purpose at the forefront of his plans. That allowed him to recognize his Defining Moment, analyze it well, and respond to it effectively. In this way, his life is a case study for the rest of us to learn from.

RESOLVE TO BE READY

Major Defining Moments don't occur *every* day; however, a Defining Moment may occur *any* day. For that reason, we need to live our lives in a manner that makes us ready for Defining Moments when we encounter them. It is always a challenge to live in a state of constant readiness. It is even more challenging when we don't know exactly what event or circumstance we will be encountering and don't know when it will arrive.

That is the nature of a major Defining Moment. It can come when you are an eleven-year-old child at a carnival, or it can come when you are a sixty-five-year-old man whose business is failing. Yet you need to be prepared at all times, because the moment that can change your life forever could arrive today! Here are some things to keep in mind as you await your next Defining Moment:

1. *Use Micromoments to Change Your Life!* As we discussed in chapter 8, you encounter micromoments regularly. These are the decisions you make in the little things in life that shape your character. Remember that always *doing the right thing,* even in seemingly unimportant decisions, will make you into a person of character. That will make it easy to make the correct decision when you are facing a major Defining Moment in your life.

2. *Realize Your Purpose!* We discussed this earlier in this chapter, but it bears repeating. Never lose sight of the fact that God has called you to a purpose and that you have a goal ahead of you.

3. *Live Your Life!* As Christians, we are to live our lives to the fullest until Christ returns. That is one of the messages of the parable of the talents. In that parable, the nobleman went away to a far country and gave his servants ten pounds and told them to, "Occupy till I come," or alternatively, "Put this money to work until I come back." The servants who put the money to work were rewarded, but the one servant who failed to do so was called a wicked servant and the money he had was taken from him![6] Frequently, our dissatisfaction with our existing situation prevents us from maximizing our daily lives. It is critical that we live life to the fullest every day. God expects us to produce results with the talents He has given us. Only then can we expect God to trust us with additional, major changes He has in store for us.

The time immediately prior to and after the birth of Christ was a time of extraordinary divine intervention on earth. Angels appeared to Mary, the mother of Christ, and to Elizabeth, the mother of John the Baptist, to tell them of the birth of their children. An angel appeared to Zacharias, the father of John. Angels appeared to shepherds to announce the birth of Christ, and a special star appeared to lead the three wise men to the newborn savior. What an amazing time to be living in Israel!

However, in the midst of all these supernatural events is the story of Anna, the prophetess.[7] Anna is the perfect example of someone waiting for her Defining Moment. The Bible tells us that she had served God in the temple with fasting and prayer for eighty-four years. With that description, she hardly seems a person that would be noticed in the world. Yet her story is recorded in the Scriptures and is a vital piece of the fabric of the story of the birth of Christ.

If you put yourself in her position, you have to imagine that during her eighty-four years of temple service there were moments of questioning her purpose. There had to be moments where she would watch the world go by and wonder what she was doing with her life. When her husband died after seven years of marriage, Anna would have been a young woman, certainly capable of remarrying and living a normal life, but that was not her calling. Rather, she committed her life to the temple ministry. I am sure that she saw friends entering and exiting the temple daily. As she did, she saw their families grow and their children and grandchildren be born and raise their own families. There had to be moments of deep loneliness and self-doubt.

Yet Anna lived a life of holiness (*i.e.*, micromoments) and stayed true to her purpose. After eighty-four years of service, when her Defining Moment arrived she was ready, and her life changed forever. The sight of Christ in the temple was that special Defining Moment in her life. The Bible tells us that in the *instant* when Anna saw the baby Jesus, she gave thanks unto the Lord and spoke of Him to all them that looked for redemption in Jerusalem. At that moment she changed, from being a widow in the temple to being an evangelist, telling all those looking for redemption that the Redeemer had arrived.

The Bible doesn't say how long Anna lived after that day, but we can be certain that she maximized the time she had left on this earth. Anna recognized the Defining Moment facing her, analyzed it, and responded in such a way that her story is still being discussed, and she remains an example to us, two thousand years later!

SEIZE THE MOMENT WHEN IT ARRIVES

Carpe diem is such a great phrase! We all love the concept of seizing the day or the moment. The term has been used and absorbed into our cultural lexicon and is generally considered a rallying cry for making the most of life. It conjures up romance and adventure.

Yet the term has more to its meaning. The phrase was used by the Roman poet, Horace, in 23 BC in the phrase, *carpe diem quam minimum credula postero,* and can be translated literally as "pluck the day, trusting as little as possible in the next one"[8] However, as much as we like using the term, if taken literally it carries a meaning that is inconsistent with achieving many of our goals in life. While we all should live to maximize each day, we need to also consider the consequences of our actions in the moment and their impact upon our futures and the lives of others around us.

The opposite of *carpe diem* is to linger, delay, defer, or otherwise do nothing. Unfortunately, when faced with a Defining Moment in their lives, many people do nothing. For one reason or another they are not willing to act and let the moment pass them by. *This is an absolute opportunity killer!* As Leonard Ravenhill said, "The opportunity of a lifetime needs to be seized during the lifetime of the opportunity." There are many reasons for this inaction, but the failure to seize upon the opportunity can result in the opportunity disappearing. It can leave us with the sense that we have left something undone and can haunt us for years.

I have a friend, we'll call him Bill. Bill had a tremendous calling on his life. He knew it, and because I knew Bill so well, I knew it. His calling was consistent with his training, spiritually, personally, and professionally. However, when an opportunity presented itself that would have allowed Bill to fulfill that calling, he was unable to pull the trigger on it. Bill had multiple reasons (*i.e.*, excuses), some of them even sounded religious, almost holy! Unfortunately, opportunities typically don't wait a long time, and Bill's opportunity was no different. Time moved on, and Bill continues to serve in the same career and capacity that he has for years. Certainly his life is nothing to be ashamed of, and most would never think that he missed out on anything. But knowing Bill, I know that a greater calling was available to him. Although we rarely see each other anymore, I think his inaction still haunts him too.

The challenge we need to meet in facing our Defining Moments is to take action quickly, yet deliberatively and decisively. When our moment arrives, we can't wait too long and cannot be frozen by inaction or overanalysis. We need to take that action, especially when that action would be consistent with our calling and our prior preparation. If we do that, our world can change instantly and become a beautiful place.

———

After law school, my wife and I moved to Dallas, and I was blessed with a great job at a large and very successful Dallas law firm. However, almost immediately, I realized that the job I had was not consistent with the career that I wanted. I looked at multiple opportunities and changed jobs twice, but all the time thought that my best career path was to start my own law firm.

Kevin was a friend from college, and although we went to different law schools, he and I joined the same law firm in Dallas. Kevin and I were kindred spirits to the extent that we wanted to open our own firm, and we explored the idea within a few years after connecting in Dallas. However, nothing seemed to be quite right. We took different jobs, but eventually ended up working together again in 1987 at the Federal Asset Disposition Association (FADA), where our jobs were to liquidate assets of failed savings and loan associations—a booming business in the late 1980s. Despite the fact that we had great jobs and were making good money, we both knew that ultimately we wanted to start and operate our own law firm. We actively planned our departure from the FADA during the summer of 1989. One day in early August of that year we were presented with the opportunity to leave the FADA in what proved to be a Defining Moment in both of our lives.

During our tenure at the FADA, Kevin and I had been fortunate to meet many Dallas real estate professionals, including one of our heroes, Roger Staubach. One day I got an unexpected call from one of Roger's associates who asked if Kevin and I would be able to go to lunch with him. Well, I didn't have to check with Kevin but accepted on the spot for both of us. During our lunch, Roger said that he had heard we were planning to start our own law firm and wondered if we could help him with a project. After discussing it, we said it was right up our alley and asked him when he needed it done. His answer was, "Two weeks!" Wow! That was not consistent with the time frame we were considering, but I said we would call him back that afternoon.

This was a textbook Defining Moment—we recognized it and the analysis was simple. We wanted to fulfill a dream of ours that had been developing for nearly a decade, to start our own law firm. Because we understood our purpose and knew our dream, we recognized the Defining Moment when it arrived. Here we were being given the opportunity for our first client to be not only the most recognizable real estate businessman in Dallas, but also one of the most admired people in the entire nation! We would never get another first client like this, and if we didn't accept the offer, we would probably not get a second opportunity to represent him.

Although we weren't prepared to leave that day when we went to lunch, we knew what we wanted and decided to act on the opportunity when it arrived. We knew it was a risk, especially since we both had wives, young children, and no safety net. In fact, within weeks after leaving our jobs I had to sell my 1978 Corvette to raise money for living expenses! However, we asked God to bless our endeavor and decided to move forward.

The response was simple—after getting the approval of the head of the FADA, we resigned that afternoon, called Roger back, and accepted the work. We found office space, hired a legal secretary, bought equipment and supplies, and opened our law firm four days later. We worked around the clock for the next ten days and finished the project on time. After that our business took off. Within a few years we had been blessed with clients and business opportunities which allowed us to develop a national real estate practice. Our response to that Defining Moment took us to places we never dreamed were possible prior to that momentous lunch. *Carpe diem,* indeed!

REJOICE AND ENJOY YOUR REWARDS

One of my favorite Bible verses is Ecclesiastes 2:24: "There is nothing better for a man, than that he should eat and drink, and that he should make his soul enjoy good in his labour. This also I saw, that it was from the hand of God." Yet this verse comes at the end of a chapter that points out the folly of pursuing a hedonistic life of eating, drinking, and making merry, and the empty vanity of accumulating wealth for its own sake. These seemingly inconsistent passages must be reconciled, and that brings us to the final point in discussing how to handle Defining Moments.

God has a plan for your life, and the purpose of this book has been to help you focus on that plan and achieve all that God has in store for you. Making sound decisions at the Defining Moments in your life will help you achieve that purpose. Finding and fulfilling God's purpose in your life will bring satisfaction, peace, and fulfillment. It *may* even bring wealth and fame. However, wherever that path takes us and whatever the blessings that accompany it, we need to be sure to enjoy the journey, from beginning to end.

We need to recognize that finding God's purpose for our lives is a blessing in and of itself. And as shown by the life of Colonel Sanders, we need to realize that it is never too late. By *recognizing, analyzing,* and *responding effectively* when we face our Defining Moments, we will walk in the path God has prepared for us. Every day lived in God's purpose is a blessing from God. Despite any challenges we face along the way, we can, and should, rejoice in the fact that we are walking in that path of His blessings. With that knowledge, we can enjoy every day God gives us, and make every day one more experience in a truly blessed life.

Now go and live that life!

AUTHOR CONTACT

If you would like to contact Lorne Liechty, find out more information, purchase books, or request him to speak, please contact:

Lorne O. Liechty
11910 Greenville Avenue, Suite 400
Dallas, TX 75243
Phone: 214-288-2854
Website: www.lorneliechty.com
Email address: lliechty1@gmail.com

ABOUT THE AUTHORS

Lorne Liechty, a graduate of Oral Roberts University and the University of Notre Dame Law School, is a business lawyer with forty years of practical experience. He is the longest-serving elder at Lakeshore Church, Rockwall, Texas, where Brad Howard is senior pastor.

Brad Howard is the pastor of Lakeshore Church in Rockwall, Texas. He is a husband, father, grandfather, and former Oreo cookie addict. His life mission is to bring hope and healing to a hurting world.

NOTES

Chapter 1

1. *Playboy* Interview: Muhammad Ali (Second Interview, 1975)
2. dictionary.com
3. Exodus 17
4. Wikipedia; Jewish virtual library.org
5. Exodus 17:9
6. Exodus 24-32
7. Numbers 13:30 (NKJV)
8. Numbers 14:36-38
9. Numbers 32:12
10. Matthew 19:16-26, Mark 10:17-27, and Luke 18:18-27
11. Matthew 19:17
12. Mark 10:21 (NKJV)

Chapter 2

1. Cardinal Newman, John Henry, "An Essay on the Development of Christian Doctrine."
2. Proverbs 11:14
3. Merriam-Webster.com
4. 1 Peter 1:6-9
5. See, *e.g.*, Jeremiah 29:11

Chapter 3

1. See chapter 9
2. Jeremiah 1:5; 29:11
3. Luke 14:23
4. Matthew 5:48
5. Psalm. 90:12
6. We won't expand the scope of our study by getting into a discussion of heaven, rewards and crowns in heaven, the translation into heaven of who we are here on earth, or any innumerable other topics this could lead to!

Chapter 4

1. azquotes.com/quotes/topics/nut-and-bolts
2. Proverbs 4:5-6
3. Ruth 2:1
4. Hebrews 11:31

Chapter 5

1 Therefore, if anyone is in Christ, he is a new creation; old things have passed away; behold, all things have become new. 2 Corinthians 5:17 (NKJV).
2 Romans 7:18-19
3 Billy Graham, *Peace With God* (Doubleday, 1953), 140-141.
4 N.T. Wright, *After You Believe* (Harper Collins, 2010), x.
5 Colossians 1:28-29 (NIV)
6 Mark 8:34 (NIV)
7 biblestudytools.com/dictionaries/bakers-evangelical-dictionary/disciple-discipleship.html
8 Matthew 6:9-13
9 Galatians 6:2
10 Hebrews 10:25
11 Hebrews 10:24 (NIV)
12 Acts 2:44-45
13 Acts 5:4
14 At one time, estimated to be the median amount of time that protestant church-goers have been attending the same church. *The Courier* (baptistcourier.com), February 20, 2007, citing a survey by Ellison Research of Phoenix, Arizona.

Chapter 6

1 Jeremiah 1:5; 29:11
2 Ecclesiastes 9:10; Colossians 3:23
3 Genesis 2:15 (NIV)
4 lexico.com
5 *e.g.,* Jeremiah 1:5; Psalm 57:2 (NLT)
6 Psalm 37:4
7 Luke 9:59-62
8 Bruce Wilkinson, *The Prayer of Jabez* (Multnomah Press, 2000), 23.

Chapter 7

1 https://www.mayoclinic.org/healthy-lifestyle/adult-health/in-depth/friend-ships/art-20044860 – August 24, 2019.
2 hrsa.gov/about/strategic-plan
3 The "Loneliness Epidemic," January 2019, https://www.hrsa.gov/enews/past-issues/2019/january-17/loneliness-epidemic.
4 *Lonesome Dove*, Simon and Schuster, 1985, McMurtry, Larry, p. 572.

5   Forbes.com, Jia Wertz, September 12, 2018.

6   Genesis 2:18

7   Genesis 2:24

8   Matthew 19:5

9   Ephesians 5:31

10 Genesis 1:28

11 Psalms 127:3

12 Mark 10:13-16

13 Proverbs 18:22 (NKJV)

14 United State Census Bureau, U.S. Marriage and Divorce Rates by State, January 15, 2020.

15 Jay L. Zagorsky, "Marriage and divorce's impact on wealth," *Journal of Sociology,* December 1, 2005.

16 Amy Morin, LCSW, "The Psychological Effects of Divorce on Children," verywellfamily.com, August 6, 2019.

Chapter 8

1   Wikipedia

2   Wikipedia

3   Luke 12:3

4   1 Samuel 17:29

5   1 Samuel 17:34-36

6   1 Samuel 17:40

Chapter 9

1   Edward N. Lorenz, ScD, "Predictability; Does the Flap of a Butterfly's Wings in Brazil Set Off a Tornado in Texas?" American Association for the Advancement of Science, 139th Meeting.

2   Sadie Dingfelder, "Reflecting on Narcissism," *Monitor on Psychology,* vol. 42, no. 2 (2011).

3   Matthew 5:13-16

4   Mark 12:31

5   Luke 1:11-20

6   Luke 1:36

7   Luke 1:16-17

8   Luke 1:67-79

9   John 3:27-30

[10] Matthew 14:1-12

[11] Luke 10:25-37

[12] 1 Corinthians 8:13 (NKJV)

[13] John 3:30

[14] John 1:15-28

[15] John 1:35-42

[16] It appears that John did have followers who remained his disciples. Matthew 11:2-3.

Chapter 10

[1] Interview with Mike McManus; https://www.tvo.org/video/archive/col-sanders.

[2] Interview with Mike McManus; https://www.tvo.org/video/archive/col-sanders.

[3] The Washington Post (December 10, 1978), p. C5; wikiquote.org/wiki/Today.

[4] Jeremiah 29:11

[5] fbijobs.gov

[6] Luke 19:11-27

[7] Luke 2:36-38

[8] Britannica.com/topic/carpe-diem